The
"How To Write *What*"
Book

The "How To Write *What*" Book

For the thousands of writers in science,
industry, government, and education
who seek a better way to present information

Harry E. Chandler

American Society for Metals
Metals Park, Ohio 44073

Copyright © 1978
by the
AMERICAN SOCIETY FOR METALS
All rights reserved

No part of this book may be reproduced, stored in a
retrieval system, or transmitted, in any form or by
any means, electronic, mechanical, photocopying,
recording, or otherwise, without the prior
written permission of the publisher.

Library of Congress Cataloging in Publication Data
Chandler, Harry E   , 1920-
  The "how to write what" book.
  1. Rhetoric.   I. Title.
PN187.C5   808'.066   78-6567
ISBN 0-87170-001-8

PRINTED IN THE UNITED STATES OF AMERICA

Preface

Having put together what is intended to be a specialized how-to book on what is (or should be) a subject of importance to a potentially vast audience, I feel an obligation to precede the text with answers to some questions:

What does the title mean? Just what it says. The spotlight is on content — more precisely, on a variety of practices that influence *what* is written, rather than on the classic how-to-write rules that do not take content into consideration.

What is the readership envisioned? Millions of do-it-yourselfers in business, industry, science, government, education, etc., who are forced to write as a part of their job or profession, who typically fear/hate every moment of it, and who do a C-minus or worse job and are probably unaware of it. Also, apprentices and other would-be authors, who will discover herein a rare opportunity to view the entire writing process laid flat out on the table.

What commends this book above all others of its kind? It is not dull or traditional or conventional.

Why was it written? To answer a question that bothered me for several years.

Why do I think I'm qualified to write this book, and what took me so long? The answers to these questions are related to the one above, as I'll proceed to explain.

In the late 1950's and early 1960's, I was totally immersed in the "how-to" aspects of writing. By day, I edited copy for a weekly business magazine that had a staff of 25 writers. Two nights a week, I taught university courses in editing and writing for business and trade magazines. At this time, I started to collect examples of good and bad writing from sources ranging from annual reports, publicity releases, and speeches to technical papers, articles from business and trade magazines, and books written for businessmen, because I couldn't find a suitable textbook. I used these bits and pieces, along with notes I had assembled, to give my lectures.

In these pursuits, from time to time I ran across blanket indictments of large segments of the population: "Businessmen are lousy writers"; "engineers are lousy writers"; "scientists are lousy writers"; "government people are lousy writers"; and so on. The charges puzzled me. In the course of my work on the magazine, I had almost daily contact with the accused. Frankly, I was impressed by many of them. Good smarts. Good judgment and common sense. Good command of the language, plus a flair for delivering an oral message in a fairly systematic manner. All signs of a latent ability to write. Yet, after long and careful study of the abundant evidence, it was hard to disagree with the critics. These people, singly and as groups, tended to be ineffective writers. Why?

For some reason, the subject attracted an inordinate amount of attention during this period, and several theories were advanced.

Some experts felt that grammar and English composition would provide the cure for ineffective writing. They reasoned that bad writers did not have a natural disposition or talent for these subjects and virtually ignored them once they got out of high school.

Another set of observers proposed that wordiness was the root of all evil; that salvation would come in the form of short words, short sentences, short paragraphs, short communications. These theorists had a great deal of credibility because they leaned heavily on numbers: "No words of more than X syllables. No sentences longer than X words."

Then there was an appealing psychological approach: "People get all puckered up when they write" was its premise; all you have to do is relax and write the way you talk.

After due consideration, I rejected all three concepts.

The secret of success hardly hinges on one's ability to distinguish a compound adjective from an adjective-adverb combination, or on one's knack for spotting and avoiding the almost universally feared split infinitive.

The short-word/short-sentence advice can work — if you are a skilled writer adept at distilling information. This style, however, can result in gibberish; also, it promotes boring oversimplification and encourages wordiness — the very thing it is aimed at avoiding.

"Write as you talk" appears to make sense until you tap a conversation. The fundamentals of proper writing — such as careful word selection, a minimum of rambling, avoidance of unnecessary repetition, and a certain sense of urgency in delivering the message — are missing.

Eventually, a fourth group of critics caught my attention. They subscribed to all the precepts of the three other schools and threw in a kicker of their own. They charged, in effect, that the scientists, engineers, businessmen, etc., are plagiarists! "That's why they seldom, if ever, have anything new or worthwhile to say."

I was interested. Not because I bought the plagiarism angle, but because these critics narrowed the inquiry to what I considered to be the essence of writing: content — what is said.

Back to the drawing board. I gathered more evidence. I gave the matter more thought. And, I must admit, I became confused. I found evidence of pilferage and theft, but I also continued to encounter all the standard problems — wordiness, inept sentence construction, shoddy word selection — which I could not account for without embracing theories I had rejected.

Furthermore, I was discouraged by conversations with peers. "It's ridiculous," they insisted, "to believe that the content part of writing is teachable."

It was at this point, around 1960, that I began the first draft of this book, armed with all my lecture notes, clippings and other research materials conscientiously gathered en route. The resulting manuscript was close to four inches thick, but it lacked a premise that satisfied me. In reviewing and pondering what I had written, I hoped I would eventually see the light at the end of the tunnel. I didn't. I let the stack of paper incubate for a couple of years, hoping that I or someone else would solve the mystery. From time to time, I'd take another stab at it, but with little success. Finally, I abandoned the project and rarely gave it any thought until about 1976. Then, on more whim than wisdom, I prodded myself into action. Perhaps this is the way it was destined to be, because the pieces fell together with hardly a struggle.

And I had found my premise. "Aha," I concluded, "it looks as if these people are stealing from each other because they are formula writers; and these formulas include standards for things like language, organization and sentence construction. All of these things have a direct or indirect influence on content."

I rewrote the first draft, reducing its length by about 75%, in about three months, writing evenings after work and during weekends — almost without letup. The thing now made sense. I was satisfied. It would, I hoped, be a useful book.

Then an unexpected thing happened: I got cold feet. I fretted, "Who am I to tell literally millions of people they can't write; that I know why; and that I can help them?"

This meant another delay. In about a year, I have convinced myself that what I have to offer is at least on a par with the other theories I'm aware of.

On this basis, I'm willing to give it a go.

HARRY E. CHANDLER

Contents

1. How To Write *What*: For By-The-Numbers Writers — 1
2. A Brief History of the Patient — 4
3. What's Wrong With Ready-Made Outlines — 8
4. Two Suitable Formats — 16
5. If There Is a Secret, This Is It — 22
6. How Writers Think — 26
7. Ready-Made Outlines Cheat You, and Your Readers — 29
8. Organization I: How Readers Read — 31
9. Organization II: Blueprint for Documentation — 33
10. Organization III: Making It Fit; Keeping It Moving — 35
11. Getting off to a Right Start — 45
12. When There Aren't Any Ready-Made Outlines — 53
13. Telling Versus Telling About — 55
14. Another View of the By-The-Numbers World — 63
15. Saying It More Than Once More Than Once — 64
16. Piling Them Up and Pennsylvania Dutch — 73
17. Circuitous Telling — 75
18. A Rubber-Stamp Language — 77
19. Science Fiction and No-Facts — 79
20. Summing Up — 82
21. Editing: Insurance for Readers — 86
22. What You Read Can Help You Write — 91

The
"How To Write *What*"
Book

Chapter 1

How To Write *What*: For By-The-Numbers Writers

The theme suggested by the flaky title and derogatory subtitle of this book requires clarification.

The analogy to painting-by-the-numbers caricatures the spectacular — but seldom acknowledged — limitations of a brand of formula writing particularly common to the voluminous literature of science, business, industry, government, and education.

"How to Write *What*" was chosen for the title to set this book apart from those taking a conventional route to the subject. What's wrong with this literature can't be cured with booster shots of grammar and English composition, or such patent medicines as "write as you talk" or "use short words, short sentences, short paragraphs." They're like trading a headache for an upset stomach. Suggested remedies should deal directly with the real source of the problem: universal practices that have a combined undesirable influence primarily on content — what is said.

By inference then, help is available. But the small print does contain an *if*. You must have enough patience to hear out the plaintiff with an open mind before you start to mount a counterattack. At that point, it's hoped, you'll repent and resolve to mend the error of your ways. This is only partly in jest. Those who need help the most seem to be the quickest to resist it.

For the record, you probably have enough grammar and composition tools to get by.

And the origin of your problem is as easy to spot as a pro basketball center at a midget's convention.

Each time you have to write, you — in fact or in effect — go to the files. If the assignment is a management or technical report, you dig up one on the same or a similar subject you or someone else wrote. If it's a technical paper for a journal or for oral presentation at a meeting or conference, you do the same. If it's a bylined article for a business or trade magazine, you do the same. If it's an essay for a learned publication, you do the same. If it's a biographical sketch for a company house organ, you do the same. And so on.

At this point, you're looking for a formula which amounts to a ready-made outline. A blueprint with a bonanza of helpful hints on what to say, how much to say, and the order in which to say it. In other words, use blue in No. 1, red in No. 2, green in No. 3, yellow in No. 4, and so on. That's writing-by-the-numbers, the first part.

The second part (sources of other formulas used when you put words on paper) can be likened to cribbing from a colleague who gets an F in a test. Although the intent is the opposite of cheating. You have a strong desire to be right.

Here's how it happens. You are inundated by this literature. You can't escape it. It is must-reading — because it is part of the job. You are also a must-writer — because it is part of the job. It's only natural that your writing is influenced by what you read.

If the third person declarative sentence is in vogue, that's what you'll tend to use when you write.

If piling up adjectives is the style in technical writing, that's what you'll tend to do.

If "increase" is universally used in preference to words that more specifically express the idea "increase," that's the word you'll tend to select in that situation.

Simply put, you are following the precedent of standards and practices common to this literature. What looks right and sounds right to you is what you are accustomed to using.

Actually, reform lies in the opposite direction.

Your writing will improve immediately if you merely stop using ready-made outlines and follow a standard that prescribes, "Don't do anything that looks right or sounds right."

Substantial improvement, however, requires an understanding of the total impact of ready-made outlines and other precedents on what is said and certain critical aspects of how it is said, plus a grasp of fundamental writing know-how.

Ready-made outlines and recommended countermeasures are explored and explained in the first two-thirds of this book. The remainder is concerned with undesirable practices and standards plus appropriate remedies.

Chapter 2

A Brief History of the Patient

Perhaps there is some comfort in the fact that writing-by-the-numbers is not a recent invention. Minimum historical inquiry has been focused on the subject, presumably because of a lack of recognition or concern.

Be that as it may, it appears that the practice had its origin in the World War I era and subsequently evolved to its present station during World War II.

If scapegoats are required, blame the Europeans and Washington. Through deduction, it is possible to speculate — with better-than-average certainty — on how the former and the latter fit into the picture.

The practice probably took root when U. S. scientists and engineers began to copy the writing styles of the much-admired Europeans. Washington got into the act during the early 1940's when it burdened with a mountain of paper work an industry bent on winning the war. The government not only legislated the style of writing under discussion but also forced both the technical and nontechnical man to join the fraternity.

These practices have flourished and proliferated over the ensuing years. Today, overcommunication via the written word has attained the status of a cardinal virtue in science, business, industry, government, and education. Millions now write regularly as part of the job or profession. In fact, these people are often judged on their literary productivity.

So what?

Well, if we accept things as they are, we are indicting all parties as incurably lousy writers.

Numerous commentators have touched upon this aspect of the subject. They are unanimously critical. They accurately identify and catalog symptoms. Yet they invariably fail to isolate the exact nature of the malady.

Here is a sampling of critiques:

Item: "The style of American scientific writing apparently changed around the end of World War I. Before World War I, the style was personal (with many I's); it was figurative (blobs of lava falling from a volcano were likened to a sheaf of arrows sprinkling to the ground); it was active; it did not use nouns as modifiers. Around 1920, the style became impersonal, literal, passive, and peppered with strings of nouns modifying other nouns, until by 1963 we find the sentence: 'Boration was effected in water,' meaning, 'We dissolved some borax.' " (Dr. Alvin M. Weinberg, former director, Oak Ridge National Laboratory.)

Item: "Of all the skills he needs, today's manager possesses least those of reading, writing, speaking, and figuring. One look at what is known as 'policy language' in large companies will show how illiterate we are." (Peter F. Drucker, *The Practices of Management,* Harper & Brothers, New York.)

Item: ". . . every survey has shown (and industrial executives know) that the technically trained person is usually a poor and inefficient writer. . . . it is generally conceded by specialists who have studied the problem that out of every 100 engineers about five can write well. The other 95 per cent are communication ineffectives." (*Better Writing,* a publication of the American Industrial Writing Institute.)

Item: "I am appalled by the almost organized, perverse inability of businessmen to understand each other. So many seem able to remain ill-informed in the midst of the biggest information explosion man has ever known. We write reams of memos. We produce sound-color motion pictures. We print newspapers. We spend millions each day for Teletype and telephone services. But still each day I am staggered by the inability of managers to make themselves heard, read, or understood. Poor communications cost billions a year in ill-conceived actions, based on misunderstanding and baseless rumors." (John B. Lawson, Aeronutronic Div., Philco Corp.)

Item: "The reader is seeking fact, point, and content. All too often he doesn't get it. Four out of five respondents [to a survey] said some of their time was wasted. Asked about what causes the waste, they blame it overwhelmingly on wordy or repetitious material. Many also complain of material 'I shouldn't have to read,' of 'poorly organized and unclear material.'" (Lydia Strong, *The Burden of Executive Reading,* based on a survey by the American Management Association.)

Item: ". . . the typical paper in the chemical literature can be cut by one-third without loss of a single concept or contribution. Moreover, when papers are so improved, they become enough clearer that about one in four can be seen to contain too little material to warrant publication at all . . ." (Robert G. Marschner and J. O. Howe, American Oil Co., in an article, "How To Train People To Write Better Reports," *Oil and Gas Journal.*)

Item: ". . . almost all industrial writing sounds like one machine talking to another. It is so impersonal that one needs only to read the subject title to fall into a deep coma . . . also, the pattern writer . . . takes a previously written paper on the same or a similar subject, substitutes new facts, dates, and numbers, and turns it in as his own writing. This has been done over such a long time that certain forms of industrial writing have changed less in 100 years than Latin." (Kenneth L. Calkins, in an article, "Industrial Writing, Untying the Giant's Tongue," *The Quill.*)

Item: ". . . if your engineering library should burn down tomorrow, it would be no great loss because within one year the substance of all that was contained in it would be footnoted and bibliographed and re-evaluated and retrospected in new issues of the same publications that went up in smoke." (*Better Writing.*)

What Does It Mean?

Obviously, when you get down to the bottom line, you are confronted by some seemingly irreconcilable conclusions.

You could argue that the critics represent the vocal minority; that they do not know what they are talking about and/or are overreacting. Yet if you take the time to review this literature in terms of the charges above and your personal experience with it, you'll have to admit: we're dealing with something that shouldn't be swept under the rug.

On the other hand, it's hard to buy the allegation that the defendants collectively write like immigrants who just got off the boat. Talk to them. Listen. Observe.

More often than not, the accused are well-trained; more often than not, they are intelligent; more often than not, they are articulate.

And remember, these are the same people who are responsible for advances that far outweigh total prior human accomplishment.

In fact, in this context there is a tendency to say, "Forget about writing, so you can continue with your more serious business." However, that's a cop-out, because the matter *is* serious and because, in truth, these people are equipped to do a decent job of communicating via the written word. You must conclude that they, like their critics, itch but don't know where to scratch.

Plan of Attack

Let's start with the primary source of the problem: ready-made outlines.

The objective is to zero in on content, the "what" part of writing. We'll be looking for better explanations of such phenomena as, "the typical paper in the chemical literature can be cut by one-third without loss of a single concept or contribution," or ". . . the almost organized, perverse inability of businessmen to understand each other."

The latter remark is particularly pertinent because we are dealing with an "organized effort" in the sense that universal practices are involved.

Chapter 3

What's Wrong With Ready-Made Outlines

Ready-made outlines are available for practically any occasion, including scientific papers, abstracts of scientific papers, reports, technical articles, speeches, learned essays, biographical sketches, a variety of announcements, press releases, advertising copy, and annual reports.

We'll concentrate on three — the scientific paper, the technical article, and the learned essay. They cover the fundamentals.

Ready-Made Outline for a Scientific Paper

Many varieties may be found. Here's a typical ready-made outline taken from a paper reporting the findings of a research project. Numbers indicate organization, the order in which the various items are presented; also note that the amount of information for each item is indicated:

1 State subject in general terms — say 50 to 100 words.
2 Review literature on previous work, same subject — up to 1000 words.
3 State subject specifically — say 25 to 50 words.
4 Describe equipment used in study — say 500 words.
5 Describe procedures used in study — say 500 words.
6 Summarize happenings during study — up to 200 words.
7 State findings — up to 50 words.

The formula provides an insight into why an unhappy reader quoted in Lydia Strong's *The Burden of Executive Reading* declared,

"When you get through reading a title that sounds intriguing, in 90 per cent of the cases you get little or nothing from the article."

Note the influence of the ready-made outline on what was said, how much was said, and the order in which it was said — including a long delay in the explicit statement of the theme.

Let's recreate a reader's experience.

We read titles first. They tell us, or should, what the writer has chosen to write about — in this instance, let's say it's "A Report on Findings in Research Project A."

We expect the writer to start discussing his subject when we reach item 1 (general statement of subject). Typically, however, we'll be at least a little puzzled after plowing through a 50-to-100-word general dissertation on a little bit of this and a little bit of that. At this point, in fact, it is not unusual to suspect that the author has abandoned his subject ("Findings in Project A") and has taken off on a new but as yet unannounced direction. In any event, the reader must read on to even be certain of the subject. Note that with this arrangement, he'll have to wait until item 3 is reached.

So item 2 (long review of literature) amounts to a further delay. A straightforward statement of "this is the subject" is still lacking.

Item 3 contains what the reader has been waiting for. But remember, it took 1050 to 1100 words just to confirm the subject, "Findings in Project A."

Now the reader expects the writer to start developing his subject.

However, items 4 and 5 are both detours. Equipment and procedures used have nothing to do with findings.

We get closer to documentation in item 6 (summary), but as in the general statement of the subject, this is typically a mixture of wheat and chaff. Some of the documentation relates to findings. Some of it is collateral (like equipment and procedures).

What the reader has been waiting for all this time is tucked away in item 7 (findings). But typically, so little is said about findings (direct documentation of the subject) that the reader feels shortchanged, particularly when you realize he waded through 2300 words to get to this point. Of the total, only 250 words (Item 3 plus item 7) provided the "point, fact, and content" he was looking for and expected.

Obviously, all but item 3, part of item 6, and item 7 can be eliminated without any loss in content — content that directly documents the subject stated in the title. In fact, item 7 provides the only unadulterated information about findings. The remainder in items 2, 4, and 5 is secondary or collateral. These items account for 2000 words.

The summary (200 words) is a mixture of direct and indirect documentation. It's possible to salvage some of it.

Now you should begin to get an idea of why ". . . the typical paper in the chemical literature can be cut by one-third without loss of a single concept or contribution."

In this instance, the ready-made outline influenced overdevelopment of what was collateral to the subject and underdevelopment of what was directly in point. It also influenced the writer to bury the statement of his subject.

In the following example, we'll see some of the same influences coupled with a strong tendency to overuse standard information (that which is generally known by readers) on a given subject.

Ready-Made Outline for a Technical Article

> Again, there are many formulas. This one is representative.
> Take a title like "New Applications for Alloy X":
> 1 Introduction: start by repeating the title in the first sentence, add a summary of impressive but "old" applications, finish off with a summary of the well-known desirable properties of Alloy X. — 75 to 100 words.
> 2 Cite two or three case histories of "old" applications of Alloy X. Discuss each in some detail. — 500 words.
> 3 Discuss standard mechanical and processing properties (summarized in item 1) in some detail. — 500 words.
> 4 List "new" applications and talk about each one briefly. — 100 words.

In this instance, the statement of the subject is not buried like that in the scientific paper. However, you see the same overemphasis on secondary documentation and underemphasis on direct documentation.

Aside from the first sentence in the introduction and item 4 (100 words), the article is woefully lacking in content.

There's a new and even bigger problem when you take into account: (*a*) people with job-involvement in "Alloy X" will read this article; (*b*) this is their field of specialization and they already know a great deal about it; (*c*) they read everything they can find on the subject; and (*d*) they read to find out what's new — to keep up with developments and trends in their field.

In this instance, these readers already know:

1. Two-thirds of the information in the introduction: impressive "old" applications and well-known desirable properties of Alloy X. Say 75 words.

2. The in-depth case histories of old applications. Five hundred words.

3. The in-depth discussion of standard mechanical and processing properties. Five hundred words.

Result: these readers have to tolerate 1075 words of warmed-over hash to find out what's new. Their reward is nominal.

Worse still, experience tells us that other authors will elect to write about "New Applications for Alloy X." They may put a slight variation of the statement of the subject in the title and the one sentence in the introduction. But they'll all tend to repeat, exactly or closely, the 1075-word rehash cited above.

Not only that, writers on other subjects of interest to the "Alloy X" readers will probably use the same type of formula.

But the poor old reader must hang in there every time in the hope of getting a crumb of what's new.

This practice suggests that writers of this school can be practically relieved of the chore by taking advantage of today's technology. A computer can handle the bulk of the assignment. Standard information (1075 words in this instance) can be cranked into a computer's memory under the appropriate title. The writer's input will be limited to a one-sentence statement of the subject and the 100 words on new applications.

This formula and others like it explain why much of this literature is as predictable as a cowboy movie and equally unoriginal.

The crime is: the writer of scientific papers and the writer of technical articles are sitting on a wealth of original information. The former was probably directly involved in the research project. The latter has at least a number of reports from the field describing new applications of Alloy X in detail.

Result: valuable information — what the reader is looking for — is withheld because of the influence of ready-made outlines. They dictate not only the scope of content, but also how much is said about each item.

Further, when you analyze the information provided (documentation of subject), you find it is amazingly literal, obvious, shallow, and nonoriginal.

The same style of documentation also predominates where the writer does not have the benefit of a storehouse of information, and he is obliged to do research and development on his topic. In this instance, we detect a spinoff influence of ready-made outlines.

The point is illustrated by the following example.

Ready-Made Outline for a Learned Essay

Take the case of the dean of a graduate school of business. He is infuriated by critics who question "the quantity and quality" of business education today and decides to write an essay on the subject for a learned journal published by a prestigious association in his field.

Going to a ready-made outline, he finds:
1 State the charge and indicate how you intend to refute it.
2 Cite, discuss, and interpret published statistics that support your position.
3 Cite, discuss, and interpret published information that supports your position.
4 Cite pertinent in-house programs and data that support your position.

The dean starts by citing a flurry of "unjustified criticism of the quantity and quality of business education today. It seems appropriate, therefore, to throw further light on the subject in general and on the program [at his university] in particular."

The statement of the subject is in the right position. There's no need to search it out.

However, the dean proceeds to "follow the script."

Predictably, he follows his statement of subject and announced plan of counterattack by taking a swipe at the quantity aspect with a recitation of standard numbers. He writes:

"The quantity of collegiate business education is easily ascertained from published statistics. For the academic year of 1960, nearly 395,000 students in the United States were awarded their bachelor's or first professional degree. When these are classified into academic groups, the field of business composes the third largest group and accounts for nearly one-seventh of the total. For men graduates only, the fraction is one-fifth. The five largest groups, in round thousands, were as follows: liberal arts, 108,000; education, 92,000; business, 53,000; sciences, including mathematics, 44,000; and engineering, 38,000 . . ."

Remember, this essay is written for people in the same field as the dean. The information is common knowledge to them. For those not in the field, it is only circumstantial evidence of "sufficient quantity."

It's apparent that the author does not have a cornucopia of "published statistics" when he practically abandons this part of the theme and concedes the "quantity" aspect of the theme when he follows the above by stating, "There are no criteria for determining whether these totals are too large or too small."

But still thinking in numbers, he gives it one last, old college try with, "It may be noted, however, that the supply of graduates is not in excess of demand at a fair wage. Current beginning salaries for graduates in business [the year is 1960] are usually from $450 to $550 per month, a figure which is higher than the rates for graduates in liberal arts and education, but a little less than the rates for scientists and engineers."

So far, it should be noted, the promised "further light on the subject" wouldn't provide too much competition for a single firefly.

Unfortunately, the dean has already hit his peak and proceeds steadily downhill when he foregoes the numbers game and resorts to standard facts from standard references to document "quality today."

He goes on, "In attempting to assess the quality of business education, there is no better way to begin than to examine its origin. Although business as a subject or program is relatively new in our educational system, it has its roots in antiquity. Socrates, it will be remembered, taught his students in the marketplace. In the Old Testament, Jethro gave Moses good instruction on organization, degradation, span of control, the exception principle, and criteria for selecting subordinate administrators — all subjects of study by modern students of business management.

"The 'handwriting on the wall' reads like an auditor's report of a defalcation and the subsequent decision in a case in bankruptcy. The New Testament contains many references to what have become subjects of study in college classes; for example, the subject of authority and how to 'speak as one having authority,' job evaluation and merit rating which seek to determine whether a 'servant is worthy of his hire,' and employee motivation and incentives which examine the problem on how to induce an employee not to 'hide his talent.' Paul's epistles to Timothy and Titus on the management of lay affairs of the church are pertinent instructions for every modern supervisor."

In the following two paragraphs, the dean reveals that an Italian Monk, Paciolo, discovered double-entry bookkeeping two years after the discovery of America; that Daniel Defoe (1661-1731), the author of *Robinson Crusoe,* wrote a book on commerce; that General Robert E. Lee was the first to establish a business curriculum for a college, while he was president of Washington and Lee; and that the Wharton School of Business (circa 1884) at the University of Pennsylvania was the first to establish a successful program.

All this, mind you, is offered as evidence of the "quality" of business education "today." At best, it is quality by historical association.

The dean now shifts to pertinent in-house programs and data (item 4 on the ready-made outline).

He rambles through long, dull descriptions of requirements for graduate degrees and describes the three main approaches to instruction (the case, quantitative, and behavioral).

Such information is available in all college catalogs.

The dean, in his parting shot at critics, lists the names of people who have received PhD's from his school and the titles of their theses; he concludes with a listing of candidates for the degree and their present positions. Significantly, not one of the doctors or candidates for the degree is in business. All except one (listed as deceased) are teaching college.

No part of the 3000-word essay sheds any visible light on either the "quantity" or "quality" of business education today.

In all fairness, the dean could have done at least 100% better by eschewing the ready-made outline and what goes with it.

Presumably, he has had years of exposure to graduates who have made their marks in business. He also knows their employers and has discussed the topic with them many times. He has reached conclusions, formed opinions, gained insights.

In light of experience, the dean could have taken a couple of different tacks.

He could have gone to graduates of his school who have been working long enough to know how well they were prepared in school.

He could have solicited a sampling of opinion on the "quantity" and "quality" of their schooling.

Or he could have gone to their employers to get their observations and opinions.

Or he could have combined the approaches.

Of course, the dean didn't do these things because he was following precedent and had no reason to question it.

The Bigger Picture

The preceding examples, which are in everyday use, represent only a small fraction of total practice. Remember:

    1. There are many variations of ready-made outlines for technical papers, technical articles, and essays (the last also serve as models for speeches).

    2. There is at least an equal number of ready-made outlines for other forms of this literature.

    3. There is always a danger of being victimized by one or more of the limitations discussed above any time you follow the example of what you, or someone else, has written. Within the sanctions of recommended practice — the subject of the next chapter — each outline should be unique.

Chapter 4

Two Suitable Formats

Two formats (one for general purposes, the other for special purposes) avoid the pitfalls discussed so far.

"Format" is used in this sense: a general plan of attack, rather than a ready-made outline that dictates what you say, how much you say, and the exact order in which you say it item by item.

The general-purpose format is suitable for most occasions, including scientific papers, technical articles, and essays. Here are the fundamentals for both general and special-purpose formats:

1 State your subject explicitly and immediately, using as many words as you need. However, keep in mind that a light touch is preferred to overkill at this point, because overwriting tends to bury or at least blur the statement of your subject.

2 After finishing step 1, go immediately to direct documentation. One tip: don't try to cover too much ground; pick your two, three, or four major points. Develop each in depth. Trying to touch all bases is a common mistake. You can't do justice to any of them. Further, now you'll have to release all the information you've been sitting on. Otherwise, you won't have much to talk about. The reader will be satisfied. He won't complain about what you left out. He wants and gets specific, in-depth information.

3 Relegate leftovers (secondary documentation) to this position. Typically, you'll see their relative unimportance at this point and either forget about them or at least minimize them. Note that the ready-made outlines discussed earlier focus primarily on information that's of secondary importance to your subject.

A Quick Review

It's instructive to take another look at the three ready-made outlines to pinpoint what is salvageable and what isn't.

The scientific paper: Start with item 3 (explicit statement of subject); then skip all but item 6 (summary of happenings) and item 7 (findings). This means you are about 2000 words short of what you need.

The technical article: Start with an exposition of your title, but keep it short and avoid summaries of old applications and standard information on desirable properties. Jump down to item 4 (new applications) and hit each one hard. Forget case histories of old applications (item 2) and the dissertation on standard mechanical and processing properties (item 3). Some critics will argue that what was omitted is necessary to make the article complete. Ignore them. Or you may hear the argument, "What about the people who are new in this field?" Remind these protectors of the status quo that textbooks are available.

The essay: There's nothing wrong with the format — in fact, it is like the general-purpose type. Lack of original information is the problem here.

Special-Purpose Format

Suppose writers of technical papers complain, "You are leaving out valuable information when you drop the review of literature, description of equipment used, and description of procedures used."

As far as the literature search is concerned, cite the comment in Chapter 2, ". . . if your engineering library should burn down tomorrow, it would be no great loss because within one year the substance of all that was contained in it would be footnoted and bibliographed and re-evaluated and retrospected in new issues of the same publications that went up in smoke."

As far as the descriptions of equipment and procedures are concerned, it should be recognized that special-interest groups have a stake in such topics. But don't burden all readers with this material. By tailoring your content (statement of subject and direct documentation), you can slant your paper or article for a specific audience.

For illustration, we'll start with a fabricated short article following the general-purpose format. Then we'll slice up the information four ways with special-purpose formats. Where it is needed, new information will be added.

> TOKYO — An electronically operated machine that eliminates the need for human operators and supervision has been installed at Sukiyaki Products Ltd., Tokyo.
>
> The machine produces a new material, called WoodSteel. It's as easy as wood to machine and as tough as steel, claims Fred Sukiyaki, president of the company.
>
> "WoodSteel," he predicts, "will be used extensively in products now made of steel wire."
>
> He continues, "This material will make it possible for us to compete with all wire products. It'll sell for about 4 cents a pound less than standard steel wire."
>
> The machine was invented by Lake Placid Research Co., Dry Gulch, N. Y. It is made under license by Export Inc., Rocky River, Tex.
>
> Mr. Sukiyaki states that no other company in the world has the machine. He declined to release further information until production data are accumulated.

Tailoring for a Company President

U. S. Grant is president of ABC Co. His company makes wire products, including birdcages. He's interested in what the competition (domestic and foreign) is doing. Here is an article (based on the general-purpose article) with information tailored for him:

> Look for a major shakeup in domestic and foreign markets this fall when a proprietary wire substitute called WoodSteel is introduced by Sukiyaki Products Ltd., Tokyo. The claim is that it can be substituted in all products now made of wire.
>
> "WoodSteel will sell for about 4 cents a pound less than wire in both the domestic and foreign markets," says Fred Sukiyaki, president of the company. "Of course, the biggest price advantage will go to countries with the lowest labor content in their products," he adds.
>
> In the United States, labor content in a standard wire birdcage is $4; materials cost another $2.

In Japan, by comparison, labor runs $1.45, materials about $1.98.

"We're able to cut the price of our material because the machine that makes it is completely automated. No operators are needed. No supervision is required," explains Mr. Sukiyaki.

The machine, said to be the only one of its kind, was invented in the United States (by Lake Placid Research Co., Dry Gulch, N. Y.) and is produced under license by Export Inc., Rocky River, Tex.

"We're willing to sell the machine to anyone," says Clarence C. Clarence, president of Export Inc. "But domestic companies have been afraid of it because of union and government pressure anytime anyone talks about eliminating jobs. Now it looks like a foreign competitor may force the issue."

The product is said to be as easy to machine as wood and as tough as steel.

Tailoring for a New Product Manager

Goldwater Barry is ABC's new product manager. He's interested in developments in all materials for birdcages and related wire products. Here's a version tailored for him:

A substitute material called WoodSteel is expected to dramatically expand the new product potential of wire fabricators. The new product can be used in all fabrications now made of wire, including birdcages.

"Greater design freedom will be offered because the material is as easy as wood to machine and as tough as steel," states the sole supplier, Sukiyaki Products Ltd., Tokyo. "Its average tensile strength is 40,000 psi; and it has an elongation of 20%."

The material will be introduced in international markets this fall. It'll sell for about 4 cents a pound less than standard wire.

Sukiyaki will not release further information until production data are accumulated.

Tailoring for a Purchasing Agent

Herman Herman is ABC's purchasing agent. He is interested in the availability and price of wire and competing materials. Here is a version tailored for him:

> A substitute that undersells wire by 4 cents a pound will be introduced internationally this fall by Sukiyaki Products Ltd., Tokyo, the sole producer.
>
> "The price includes all shipping and handling costs," explains Fred Sukiyaki, president of the company. "We expect to have distribution points on both coasts of the United States and in the Midwest in operation by this fall. We are not ready to pin down delivery dates at this time."
>
> It's possible that other sources may open up. The machine that makes WoodSteel is being offered internationally by Export Inc., Rocky River, Tex.

Tailoring for a Production Manager

G. Lombardo is ABC's production manager. He is interested in machines that make wire and wire products. Here's a version of the article tailored for him:

> An electronically operated machine that eliminates the need for human operators and supervision has been installed at Sukiyaki Products Ltd., Tokyo. It produces a wire substitute called WoodSteel.
>
> "We'll be able to cut our hourly labor costs by $1-million within 18 months," predicts Fred Sukiyaki, president of the company. His firm is said to have the only installation in the world, but the machine is available from Export Inc., Rocky River, Tex.
>
> "We're willing to sell the machine to anyone," says Clarence C. Clarence, president of the Texas firm. "But domestic companies have been afraid of it because of union and government pressures anytime anyone talks about eliminating jobs. Now it looks like a foreign competitor may force the issue."
>
> WoodSteel, said to be as easy as wood to machine and as strong as steel, will be introduced in international markets

this fall. "It'll sell for about 4 cents a pound less than wire," says Mr. Sukiyaki.

The company declines to release further information until production data are accumulated. WoodSteel is expected to be used extensively in products now made of wire.

A Few Comments

That's tailoring.

In this instance, four different versions of the basic article for four different special-interest groups within the same company.

Some common information is used in each example. However, where it is presented within the article depends upon the special interest of the reader. New information was required for each type of reader.

Obviously, the writer of the tailored articles was forced to analyze and evaluate all of his available material, then select it on the basis of the type of reader involved.

The "thinking" aspect of writing will be discussed in the next two chapters.

Chapter 5

If There Is a Secret, This Is It

If there is any proprietary writing know-how to divulge, it involves what happens, or should, in the step preceding putting words on paper. This is perhaps the least understood and most difficult phase of the writing process. It involves thinking-through your raw materials — taking inventory — in sufficient detail for you to understand them thoroughly.

A number of benefits are realized, including:

1. You can find out if you have enough material to start writing. If you conclude that you have, you pick up the self-confidence and enthusiasm required for you to do a creditable job. Doubt — particularly at this stage — is the writers' enemy No. 1. By nature, writing is partly a self-critical process. When there is too much doubt, you become overcritical and get bogged down. You'll have to pay dearly in frustration to get out of the gloom. Finally, if you believe you are lacking in raw materials, you have two options at this point: do more research and development, or drop the project if it appears you are drilling a dry hole. Unfortunately, the latter decision is avoided close to 100% of the time.

2. You should have enough of a grasp of your subject after taking inventory to state it roughly in a title or a brief paragraph. This is a milestone event for the writer. Strange as it may seem, if you are in a position to do this properly, going the rest of the way is often a piece of cake. Con-

versely, a premature start here amounts to throwing yourself to the alligators.

3. You should be in a position to make a first screening of your documentation, which will give you an idea of how much you have to say, how much primary documentation you have, which major points you should select, and which secondary documentation may be worth salvaging.

Once in a great while, inventory-taking isn't necessary. This doesn't mean you've bypassed the step; it means that all the pieces in the puzzle fell into place as you gathered and assembled your raw materials.

Ready-made outlines, as the name implies, practically eliminate inventory-taking. Critical concerns are limited to following the prescription of the formula.

Also, conventional outlines should be avoided prior to inventory-taking. You do not know enough about your material. If you start writing too soon, you'll run into a surplus of trouble all along the way because, in effect, you'll be doing more inventory-taking (accepting and rejecting, making false starts, having second and third thoughts) than writing.

There's also the possibility that you can come up with a substandard but workable outline at this point. You'll be able to complete the job, but it won't be anywhere near what you actually have available in both quantity and quality.

How To Take Inventory

Several techniques are available. All have the same dual objective: to get your thinking into writing gear (more about this in the next chapter) and to force you to take inventory. Among the techniques are writing a fast first draft, writing a fast brainstorming draft, dashing off a letter to a friend, talking it over with a friend, and formulating a title or a short statement of your subject.

The Recommended Technique

A fast brainstorming draft is recommended for nonprofessional writers. In writing a conventional fast first draft there is a constant danger of hitting cul-de-sacs and becoming unnecessarily grim about the whole matter. For one thing, you stand a good chance of not getting past the formulation of your subject, because this is such a key item; and you probably haven't sorted out your documentation well enough to separate the primary from the secondary and just plain loose ends.

In doing a fast brainstorming draft (a special type of partial inventory), the first objective is to relax. Forget all rules. Don't concern yourself with how you'll state your subject or what documentation you have. Start anyplace — beginning, middle, end; it's immaterial. But be quick. Write. Write. Write. Use the first word that comes to mind. Don't be critical. Ramble. This is for fun.

Sooner or later, by the second, third, ninth page, your thinking will slip into writing gear. You'll know you've arrived when you dig up your first nugget — it may be your subject, or a point you'll want to cover.

What you have actually done is reached the point where you can take an orderly inventory. Obviously, you aren't finished.

Two options are open:

> 1. Tear up what you've written so far and try a first draft. But if you do this, hold up on your outline until you have finished your first draft. Then do a second draft.
>
> 2. Keep going until you've completed your inventory. Write your outline from your inventory. *Then* write — this will amount to your second draft.

Sometimes you aren't certain whether you have gone far enough to take the first option. Here's where an exercise can be used as a test: try to formulate your title or a short statement (say a paragraph) of your subject. If one or the other comes easily, you are probably ready. If you encounter many false starts, continue your inventory.

Don't forget: Getting your thinking into writing gear normally takes time. So does inventory taking. The techniques being outlined merely speed up both processes.

Other Techniques

The chief benefit of dashing off a letter to a friend is that it may help you relax. Try to explain what you plan to write about, your subject, your documentation. This is merely a variation of a brainstorming draft. So is talking it over with a colleague; however, the latter has some important side benefits.

A business-magazine editor noted for his provocative editorials refined the talking technique to perfection. Two or three days before his deadline, he would have a rough idea and an assortment of thoughts about it.

From that time until the morning he had to write, any colleague passing his office was likely to be tapped for conversation about his upcoming editorial. More often than not, the colleague thought he was being invited to take part in a bull session.

Typically, the editor would start with something like, "Say, what do you think of this?" Or, "Have you noticed that?" Then he briefed his listener. The editor was forcing himself to think through his material. Each time he called in a colleague, he refined and re-refined his message.

But the listener was more than a pawn. The editor knew and took advantage of the fact that listeners also make contributions. They ask questions, which have to be answered or defended. They make direct contributions. They suggest things that have been overlooked or rejected as being unimportant.

By the time the editor's deadline rolled around, his editorial was written. All he had to do was put it on paper.

Despite the benefits of the talking-through technique, the next logical step — dictating a first draft — is not recommended. Listen to a tape or the unedited transcript of a meeting, for example.

Talking is an undisciplined process. We ramble, start, stop, back up, detour. We use the first word that comes to mind. At this level, talking is a highly ineffective method of communication.

What you'll get on tape is one step removed from conversation. It is conversation in the abstract. The face-to-face environment is missing. In speaking with a colleague or to a group, you have several extras going for you. So do your listeners. Both speaker and listener get valuable assists from such things as facial expressions, voice inflections, gestures, even meaningful silences. Elements that can be captured on only a video tape.

The well-worn advice, "Write as you talk," is ridiculous. Eavesdrop on a conversation. No one in his right mind would choose to write the way he talks. We'd like to talk the way we write.

For one thing, we can talk without careful thinking. Writing requires a mixture of disciplined and meditative thinking. We'll be talking about this in the next chapter.

Chapter 6

How Writers Think

Paradoxically, great writers spend infinitely more time on, and feel more insecure about, inventory-taking and related matters than the hacks, apprentices, and amateurs. It's instructive to learn how much they are willing to pay for their "gift."

Listen, for example, to the late Sinclair Lewis:

"I start by assembling notes. I go through them a couple of times. Soon I can't wait to get the thoughts out of my head and down on paper. So I write. I write continuously, almost, until the first draft is done. Then I sit back and wait. Or I busy myself with another task. Anything to get my conscious mind off the subject and my unconscious mind on it.

"Only after a day or two or three am I ready for step two. This time I go through the write-up slowly and carefully, page by page, adding all thoughts I left out the first time.

"Then I wait another day or two or three. Then I go through the entire story again, sentence by sentence, deleting all unnecessary words.

"Then another day's wait — and another go-through — this time editing to make everything sound like I just dashed it off.

"Four drafts! Careful, painstaking, time-consuming drafts. With time between them to allow my thoughts to simmer. I can't think of any other way of creating truly readable writing."

Note: letting the subconscious mind work on what we have is an implicit part of the process whether we are writing fiction or a technical article or a learned essay.

Another great writer, playwright Tennessee Williams, takes an extreme view on the time requirement. It was presented in *Time* magazine:

> "The only religion that works for Williams is his writing, and he practices it four hours a day, day in, day out, year in, year out, as if he had taken a vow of discipline. . . . he has no set output and contends that 'out of a year's writing days, there are only five good ones.' "

Williams had this to say about the subconscious mind: "It takes five or six years to use something out of life. It's lurking there in the unconscious — it finds meaning there."

In an article, "How Writers Write" (*Saturday Review*), author Malcolm Cowley commented:

> "Meditation may be, or seems to be, wholly conscious . . . or most of the process, including all the early steps, may be carried on without the writer's volition. . . . most frequently, I think . . . meditation is a mixture of conscious and subconscious elements.
>
> "Often, the meditation continues while the writer is engaged in other occupations, gardening, driving his wife to town, or going out to dinner.
>
> " 'I never quite know when I'm not writing,' said the late James Thurber. 'Sometimes my wife comes up to me at a dinner party and says: "Dammit, Thurber, stop writing!" She usually catches me in the middle of a paragraph.' "

Starting the process of thinking like a writer is a chronic problem. A number of name writers have developed work habits that give them the necessary assist.

Thurber, Cowley reports, found that he could start his thinking by sitting down to his typewriter. Hemingway got the same result while observing his daily ritual of sharpening 20 pencils. Willa Cather read the Bible. Others, including the late Thomas Wolfe, took long walks.

No method works all the time. Jean Kerr, the playwright, often develops an allergy to the typewriter and switches to a pencil. The typewriter scares her because the end product looks so final. She is afraid of making mistakes — strains and frets more than usual, slowing down her natural pace.

Writers work at different speeds. Many, like the late Sinclair Lewis, dash off a fast first draft and reserve self-criticism for a later time. Others can't skip the process and write laboriously.

Cowley quoted William Styron, "I seem to have some neurotic need to perfect each paragraph — each sentence even — as I go along."

The late Dorothy Parker told Cowley it took her six months to write an article. "I think it out and then write it, sentence by sentence, on first draft. I can't write five words but that I change seven," she said.

Cowley adds, "The professional writers who dread the act of writing . . . are usually those whose critical sense is not only strong but unsleeping, so that it won't allow them to do even a first draft at top speed. They are in most cases the bleeders who write one sentence at a time, and can't write it until the sentence has been revised."

He continues, "Thurber revises his stories by rewriting them from the beginning, time and again. 'A story I have been working on,' he says, 'was rewritten 15 complete times. There must have been close to 240,000 words in all the manuscripts put together, and I must have spent 2000 working hours on it. Yet the finished story couldn't be more than 20,000 words.'"

Frank O'Connor goes farther: "I keep rewriting," he says, "and after it is published in book form, I usually rewrite it again."

A Look Ahead

In the next chapter we'll take a brief look at another ready-made outline as a review and as an introduction to other phases of the writing process.

Chapter 7

Ready-Made Outlines Cheat You, and Your Readers

Perhaps the major disadvantage of a ready-made outline is that the writer excludes content not called for by the formula. In effect, he saves the feathers and throws away the chicken.

The ready-made outline for biographical sketches is particularly limiting. In form, it is analogous to a job application. Although the aim is to provide insights into the qualities of a person, it is limited in scope to bare facts and numbers, such as date of birth, schooling, job history, marital status, and number of children.

A beautiful illustration is provided in a *Sports Illustrated* article about Justice Byron R. White, "A Modest All-American Sits on the Highest Bench," by Alfred White. The author took excerpts from Justice White's official government biography as a springboard for a part of his article. Here's how a government by-the-numbers writer treated the unusual scholar-athlete:

> "He graduated from the University of Colorado in 1938, ranking first in his class of 267. . . . Mr. White was elected to the Phi Beta Kappa honorary society and was active in college activities, including varsity athletics, and was president of the Students Association in 1937-38. In 1937, he was selected as a member of the All-America football team, and in 1954 was named to the National Football Hall of Fame."

The author comments:

"Those bald statements envelop some singular feats. For instance, White won his Phi Beta Kappa key in his junior year. He won three varsity letters in football, four in basketball, and three in baseball. In his junior year he began to attract a great deal of local publicity as a triple-threat tailback on the football team, and a local sportswriter, Leonard Cahn, christened him with the catchy name of Whizzer.

"As Whizzer White, the Justice began to get national publicity, due in no small part to the journalistic attentions of Grantland Rice. During his final season he was the leading ground-gainer and leading scorer in football, and he averaged 31 yards on each of his punt returns. He scored 13 touchdowns, 19 conversions, and kicked the only field goal he attempted. He and his teammates were unbeaten and untied and went to the Cotton Bowl to play Rice on New Year's Day. During the first 10 minutes of that game White ran for a touchdown with an intercepted pass, threw a pass for another Colorado touchdown, and kicked two extra points to give his team a 14-point lead. After that, the heavier Rice squad wore down Colorado and won the game 28-14."

It's obvious that a user of ready-made outlines could not write that way if someone pointed a gun at him.

For one thing, he probably wouldn't know enough about organization to tell his story in a systematic manner.

Chapter 8

Organization I: How Readers Read

Remember the reader who complained about being seduced by intriguing titles but felt bamboozled 90% of the time after reading an article?

If you asked him to pinpoint the problem, he would probably reply, "Lack of content."

Inept organization was actually the source of his problem.

This reader and millions like him are inundated with this literature. They try to be selective.

The title is their first clue. They won't go on if it doesn't look as if there is something in it for them.

If the answer is a "go," the reader next looks for amplification of the title in the statement of the subject.

He is in a holding pattern until he finds it. Once more, he'll bail out if the literature doesn't look as if it'll be worth his time.

The reader who elects to stick with it next starts to look for solid direct documentation of the subject.

Invariably, he is forced to wade through the entire piece because direct and indirect documentation are hopelessly blended.

More often than not, the reader must go to the last word before he can determine, "This isn't for me. Why did I waste my time?"

Again, the answer is, "inept organization."

The basics cover these points:

1 Write the best-possible title, but make the statement of your subject self-sufficient. Don't count on help from the title.
2 Start direct documentation immediately after statement of sub-

ject is completed. Don't do anything to delay this start.
3 Develop your documentation in a systematic manner. (More about this in the next chapter.)
4 Put all secondary documentation at the end, or drop it.

Finally, remember that the busy reader has three opportunities to be selective: the title, statement of subject, and start of documentation. Putting him in a position to conclude, "No, I shouldn't be reading this," is at least equal in value to providing him with interesting, worthwhile information.

Chapter 9

Organization II: Blueprint for Documentation

The first rule in documentation is: Don't attempt to tell all. Pick a few key points (the number is up to your best judgment, but generally three or four will do).

The second rule: Do a careful job of developing each point in depth.

The third rule: Proceed in a systematic manner. The key to doing this is to develop each point in its entirety before going to the next one.

Say you select A, B, C. A common fault is that you give a smattering of "A," jump briefly to "C," take a swipe at "B," then return to "A" to finish it up.

The fourth rule: You can start with A or B or C. It doesn't make any difference as long as you finish one before going to the next one.

An additional step is considered good practice: summarize your key points in a short paragraph immediately after you have finished stating your subject.

This gives you an order to follow — two, in fact. With an A, B, C situation, you can start with C and work backward; or start with A and work forward.

Previewing both your documentation and your organization helps the reader. He gets tips on what to expect. If you start with "A," he expects you to follow with "B" and "C." If you start with "C," he expects "B" then "A."

The scheme is simplistically stated as, "Tell them what you'll tell them; then tell them."

The over-all objective and what to avoid are spelled out in another comment from the American Management Association study cited in Chapter 2:

"If the subject is developed step by step, the reader's interest won't be lost along the way. Unfortunately, most writers are too close to their subject to realize that the reader has to be led into it gradually and logically. As often as not, the writer starts somewhere in the middle, proceeds in a certain direction, retraces his steps to fill in some details, proceeds in a different direction, inserts another flashback, and so on."

The situation can be avoided in part by minding your ABC's. Continuity is the other half.

Chapter 10

Organization III: Making It Fit; Keeping It Moving

"That's so simple I could have written it myself."
When a reader says that, the writer has arrived.
It means he observed his ABC's of organization.
It also means he fulfilled the two basic requirements of continuity: pertinence and progression.
Pertinence relates to story logic. ("Story" is used as an alternative for paper, articles, etc.) In his title and statement of subject, the writer promises to talk exclusively about "X" topic. Everything he writes must fit, or be made to appear to fit, his title-subject. He fails when the reader must stop and ask: "What does this have to do with X?"
Progression relates to development of subject. The writer must constantly move forward, or at least give that impression. He fails in this respect when he does something that stops or interrupts continuity.
Pertinence and progression must be maintained from sentence to sentence — from the first to the last.

Example of Impertinence

A writer states he will analyze shifts in auto-buyer preferences by price categories.
He should have used sales statistics by price categories as evidence.
He chose to use production figures by price categories.
In this instance, the reader is forced to stop and observe: "The evidence does not appear to fit. At best, this is only circumstantial

evidence of auto-buyer preferences. Historically, sales lag production."

The reader was looking for, but didn't get, something like, "Two million cars in the $4000 to $5000 category were sold during the first six months of this year, compared with 1.8 million during the same period last year."

At the least, the writer should have taken one more step to make his documentation fit his topic. For example, "Sales statistics for the latest period are not available, but we can draw conclusions from production figures. They typically run about 100,000 ahead of sales in a given category."

This example suggests a guideline: The writer must ask from sentence to sentence, "Does this fit the subject?" "If it does, but doesn't appear to the way I've handled it, how can I make it fit?"

Inconsistency in logic or fact (which goes beyond story logic) can also stop the reader. Each statement must be logical in itself, and it must be consistent with everything else in the story. Each fact must be right in itself and be consistent with other facts in the story.

Example of Inconsistent Logic

"Baseball pundits predict Joe E. Brown will win the American League batting championship this year. He hit .309 last year and was ninth in the year-end standings.

"The colorful Californian drives a pink Cadillac."

A question of pure logic — as opposed to story logic — arises. Logically, Brown's taste in cars has nothing to do with his prowess at the plate.

The last sentence is impertinent as it stands. It should be eliminated, or made to conform with logic in some way.

For example, "The colorful Californian drives a pink Cadillac. Pink has been the favorite color of all previous batting champs in the American League."

Such clinkers are tougher to spot — for the writer, but not the discerning reader — when they are widely separated.

Say we write, "Brown's average (.309) put him in ninth place among American League hitters last year. He is currently hitting .347, with only one month of the season left. If he maintains the pace, and he's confident about it, he will wind up the season in the top spot."

Fifteen paragraphs later we add, "Brown told reporters in a recent interview, " 'I don't see how I can do better than I did last year.' "

An obvious contradiction of fact.

As a lot, writers tend to be indifferent mathematicians. Particularly watch such things as percentages and proportions where it's obvious to a sharp-eyed reader that the writer blew it.

Examples of Nonprogression

Progression is also concerned with such things as logic and facts.

The most common problems with progression (establishing and maintaining a sense of forward movement) arise when the writer is starting a new paragraph and is taking off on a new, but unannounced, tack.

In this sense, progression is concerned with ways to make such announcements. The technical term is *transition*, or *bridge*.

Take the case where a contrasting statement in the second paragraph calls for a transition:

First paragraph: "Your story in the July issue certainly made some good points, and I'm all for better writing."

Second paragraph: "The example given near the beginning brings up the danger of playing too fast and loose with imagery."

Note that the first paragraph is complimentary. Until you reach "danger" in the second paragraph, there is no reason to suspect that the writer is not continuing in the same vein.

A transition word like "but" or "however" is needed at the beginning of the second paragraph.

When the discerning reader reaches "danger," he will probably back up and reread the first paragraph to see if he missed something. The writer shouldn't force him to do this.

Another example:

"At the 18th annual meeting of the Mars Rocket Association, Fred Smith reported, 'Depending on the vehicle mission, the estimated cost reduction per pound of weight saved ranges up to $10,000.'

" 'Vacuum encountered in space does not restrict the use of standard magnesium alloys,' stated Paul M. Paul of XYZ Company."

Same problem as in the previous example. Until you reach Paul M. Paul, you assume that Fred Smith is still talking. The reader who does some detective work is surprised to learn that two speakers are in the act.

A transition is needed. Something like, "In a second paper, Paul M. Paul of XYZ Company, reported that the vacuum encountered in space does not restrict the use of standard magnesium alloys."

Progression and pertinence are related. If lacking, both stop the reader, but in different ways.

Some Basics for Pertinence

Always assume the reader is logical.

When a statement is not clear to him, or more than one interpretation is possible and the one intended is not indicated, this means:

    1. The writer does not understand what he is writing about — more thinking on his part is required.

    2. The writer knows what he wants to say but does not get it all on paper. He may be reading-in what he omitted; the message is clear to him. He must remember that what we put on paper is beyond recall, amendment, correction, or explanation. In other words, what he writes must be self-sufficient.

    3. The writer does not take into account the alchemy that can take place when he puts a group of words on paper. New meanings — meanings not intended by the writer — can emerge.

Here's an example of where a writer stopped thinking too soon and wrote:

> "From the various sources of project ideas, a priority is established according to which project offers the most lucrative potential in terms of cost savings."

There appears to be a connection between the phrase starting, "from the various sources . . ." and the message following the comma. There is none — as stated.

After further thinking, the writer came up with:

> "Project ideas from all sources are studied in terms of general merit. Those that survive the test are given a priority in terms of their cost-saving potential."

The reader, in addition to being logical, also judges what we put on paper in terms of his knowledge and everyday experience. For example, a reader with knowledge of elements would be stopped by this:

"New elements numbered 104 and 105 are in scientists' plans for the next underground nuclear explosion. Immediately after the blast, core drillings will be made in the neutron-enriched earth."

What the writer meant, but didn't get on paper:

"New elements numbered 104 and 105 are expected to be byproducts of the next underground nuclear explosion. Immediately after the blast, they will be looked for in core drillings made in the adjoining neutron-enriched earth."

Reading-in is an occupational hazard. The writer gets close to his material; he assumes that he puts everything on paper. In fact, he often leaves gaps.

For example:

"Storage yards are cluttered with equipment that was bought in haste. But ill-conceived purchases are rarer when a lot of money is involved."

After the writer was quizzed, he came up with this:

"Storage yards are cluttered with equipment costing $5,000 to $10,000 because there is a tendency to buy it without too much thought to its long-range usefulness. A lot more care is taken when equipment runs $50,000 to $100,000."

It should be pointed out that the writer didn't have to dig up the new information. He already had it.

Writers do not resent such criticism. However, they have little time for nitpickers who can't see beyond the literal. There are times, though, when writers *should* pay attention to nitpickers, particularly when words do not behave as-intended when they are put on paper.

Example:

"Workers at an electric steel plant less than 10 years old accepted a two-year contract."

The plant — not the workers — is 10 years old.

Example:

"Despite the terrorism and the elections slated for late this year in Venezuela . . ."

Sounds like the "terrorism" is planned.

Example:
"The company runs articles in its house organ urging older employees to plan for their retirements."
Sounds like older workers are being forced out, even though the company is merely recommending foresight.
Example:
"No one can exhibit at this show . . . if he has exhibited in any other unauthorized show."
Sounds like the only authorized unauthorized show.
Example:
". . . the ghostlike operator's gloves."
Is the operator or his gloves "ghostlike"?

Some Basics for Progression

One test for progression is to ask: does the story flow smoothly from sentence to sentence?

If you have to stop and ask: "What does this have to do with what was said in the last sentence?" you have a progression problem. A transition, or bridge, that indicates a connection with what preceded is needed. Transitions are often required when you start a new paragraph.

Devices for achieving progression include:
1. Use of a tack word, such as "this," "that," "but," "however," "meanwhile."
2. Repeating a word or words from the preceding sentence.
3. Restating or repeating an idea in the preceding sentence.
4. Indicating that something will follow.
5. Setting up a chronology and following it.
6. Following a general statement with specifics.
7. Answering a question — direct or indirect — raised by the preceding sentence.
8. Letting suggestion work for you.
9. Delivering on a promise — direct or implied — made in the preceding sentence.
10. Anticipating reader reaction to what was said in the preceding sentence.

Examples of No. 1 — Use of tack words:
"Scientific and technological development must be an-

ticipated and prepared for in advance. *This* will serve a dual purpose."

Comment: Use tack words with discretion. They can be a haven for lazy thinkers. In the last example, "The approach" would have been an improvement over "this." Tack words are overused. They promote dullness, particularly when a piece is peppered with "this" and "that."

They can also tend to slow down progression, because they can be used in a mechanical, by-the-numbers manner.

Take this example:

"Free World deliveries hit an all-time high. *This* sent producer stocks tumbling."

Two alternatives have potential for improvement (a smoother transition).

First, drop "this":

"Free World deliveries hit an all-time high. Producer stocks tumbled."

Comment: One thought flows logically into the next. A tack word isn't needed. In fact, it gets in the way. Tedious writers overuse tack words because they're afraid the reader is dense and won't get the connection.

Second possibility: combine the two sentences into one.

"Free World deliveries hit an all-time high, sending producer stocks tumbling."

Tip: Every time you use words like "thus," "therefore," "so," "meanwhile," "this," or "that," ask: Is the transition necessary? Am I overusing tack words? Also consider the possibility of dropping tack words and being more explicit.

Example of No. 2 — Repeating a word or words from the preceding sentence (the example is from *Time*):

"Joan Sutherland demonstrated even to the doubter that she is the most accomplished technician in all opera.

"Sutherland is not necessarily the best singer or the most compelling actress."

Comment: Repetition, like tack words, can be easily overused. Repetition has an added disadvantage: it refers back in effect; it is like a stop or pause. This becomes particularly noticeable if the device is used over and over or without taste. Keep in mind that alternatives are available.

Example of No. 3 — Repeating or restating an idea in the preceding sentence (another example from *Time*):

> "In the bible of Communism, hangmen are as tender as mothers. 'The doublethink of Communism,' says the author . . ."

Comment: "Doublethink" is a restatement of "hangmen are as tender as mothers." This is always a safe device; but it requires more thinking by the writer than "this" or "that."

Example of No. 4 — Indicating that something will follow:

A device as simple as a colon (see preceding sentence) does this. The ABC summary mentioned in Chapter 9 does this on a larger scale. It informs the reader that A, B, C or C, B, A will follow.

Example of No. 5 — Setting up a chronology and following it. The example is from *Reader's Digest*. Key words that indicate chronology have been italicized by me:

> "The *morning* of March 15 was pleasant and sunny as William Miner, a farmer near Center, N. D., completed his chores. A thaw had set in, and the snow in the fields was patchy.
>
> " 'Snow should be gone by night,' he reported optimistically to his wife when he came in at *noon. After the couple had eaten a leisurely meal,* Miner glanced out at the wind. 'Good Lord!' he exclaimed.
>
> "In the northwest, a black, billowy cloud loomed over the horizon. It moved stealthily, inexorably, its dark bluish edges spreading across the sky toward the unsuspecting sun.
>
> "Blanche Miner spoke with the sure instinct of a homesteader. 'A spring norther!'
>
> *"They watched the advance of the formless, faceless monster.* Abruptly, Miner said, 'You get the stock in. I'm going to school to get the kids.' "

Comment: Note how the simple chronology denotes the passage of time, a device which maintains the illusion of moving forward.

Example of No. 6 — Following a general statement with specifics:

> "The hammer has two parts: a handle and a head."

Example of No. 7 — Answering a question — direct or indirect — raised by the preceding sentence:

"Opening of the Lakeland Freeway east from E. 152nd Street to Painesville will not take place today, according to state highway officials.

"Unseasonable snow and wet weather have delayed completion of certain segments."

Comment: A question raised indirectly in the first sentence is answered in the second.

Example of No. 8 — Letting suggestion work for you. (Another example from *Reader's Digest*):

"Although I have studied nature carefully for more than 60 years, I have never been able to preconceive how wild things will react to certain circumstances. Their behavior cannot be foretold, pigeonholed, and dismissed anymore than that can be done for human beings. What is considered normal behavior is constantly being violated by the children of nature — especially if danger seems imminent."

Comment: Note how the situation set up by the author begs for examples. He obliged immediately.

Example of No. 9 — Delivering on a promise — direct or implied — made in the preceding sentence:

"You can do something about vote fraud.

"Six approaches are open to an aroused citizenry:

"1. Help build the precinct organization in your political party.

"2. Etc."

Comment: There's an implied promise in the first sentence: the writer will talk about what can be done about vote fraud. He starts to deliver in the next sentence ("Six approaches are open."). Then he uses the colon device to set up an ABC-type summary (tells the reader what he will tell). From that point on, he starts to tell, proceeding with item 1 and moving forward, or starting with item 6 and going in reverse order.

Example of No. 10 — Anticipating reader reaction to what was said in the preceding sentence or the preceding part of the piece:

Let's go back to No. 7, where the first paragraph raised a question, which was answered in the second.

"Opening of the Lakeland Freeway east from E. 152nd Street to Painesville will not take place today, according to state highway officials.

"Unseasonable snow and wet weather have delayed completion of work in certain segments of the highway, particularly in that section from East 250th to East 275th."

Comment: At this point, the writer can anticipate that the reader will want to know what work hasn't been completed. In this instance, the writer obliged with:

"Lack of berms, leaving a 12-to-15-inch dropoff on each side, would endanger motorists on the as yet unlighted road."

Chapter 11

Getting off to a Right Start

In the correct order of writing events, statement of subject is the first element in organization. I have bypassed it until now because its discussion is more meaningful within the context of the ABC principle and continuity devices.

For brevity, let's adopt the term "lead" in place of "statement of subject." It is approved journalistic jargon; this, in turn, suggests an amplification. The term "subject" has been used as a convenience. In leads, we state subjects or themes.

So much for ground rules.

Now for the nitty-gritty of lead writing.

Remember the cardinal rule: The lead is always the first element.

Ideally, it should be the first sentence in your lead, or the sum total of your first paragraph. There are approved exceptions, but you do not have the latitude to bury your lead by wandering aimlessly for two, three, or four paragraphs.

Don't make the reader look for the lead. Give it to him.

17 Lead-Writing Techniques

The following techniques have both advantages and disadvantages. Look upon them as ways to solve lead-writing problems, not merely as devices that give you variety. Both points will be self-evident in the examples that follow the list.

Here are the names of the techniques:
  1 Declarative leads.
  2 Question leads.

3 Question-answer leads.
4 Problem-solution leads.
5 Summary leads.
6 Upside-down summary leads.
7 Promise-of-benefit leads.
8 Prediction leads.
9 Interpretive leads.
10 Straight-quotation leads.
11 Famous-quotation leads.
12 Cliché leads.
13 Play-up-the-urgency leads.
14 Challenge-the-reader leads.
15 Getting-the-reader-involved leads.
16 "You" leads.
17 Incident or case-history leads.

Example of No. 1, declarative leads:
    CLEVELAND (AP) — Marvin Smith says his long-term contract with the Cleveland Browns was breached when he was removed as head coach and general manager and that the matter now is in the hands of his lawyers.

Comment: The most widely used and safest type of lead — if you have what you want to say down pat; otherwise, there's a tendency to ramble as you circle around your subject or theme. If you don't encounter too many false starts, keep trying until you have it. Otherwise, examine other techniques that may solve your problem.

Example of No. 2, question leads:
    CLEVELAND (AP) — Will Marvin Smith contest his dismissal as head coach and general manager of the Cleveland Browns?
    "Yes," says Smith, who claims his contract has been breached.
    "The matter," he adds, "has been turned over to my lawyers."

Comment: Essentially the same information as that in the declarative lead, but an important extra has been added. You raise a question. The reader automatically goes for the answer. It's a legitimate gimmick. There's a lot of show biz in writing. Also note:

the information in quotes picks up added authority. Smith, in this instance, not the writer, is doing the talking. There's no question about believability, which can be a problem with the third person declarative, particularly where your message is heavy. You can get away with things in quotes that you can't with third person declarative. An important consideration, because credibility is essential.

Example of No. 3, question-answer leads:
> Question: What can be done to lessen strife between labor and management?
> Answer: Play up common objectives instead of chronic differences, advises Jesse James, president of ABC Corporation.

Comment: Can be a problem-solver, particularly if you have trouble finding the handle on your lead, or have trouble stating it in a conventional manner. This is a variation of the question lead. Another variation is next.

Example of No. 4, problem-solution leads:
> Problem: the continuing strife between labor and management.
> Solution: "It's time for both sides to realize they have much more in common than they do in controversy," suggests Jesse James, president of ABC Corporation.

Comment: Both this and the question-answer techniques are particularly suitable for technical articles; they make it easy to put what counts out front in a hurry. Note the first part, "problem," in particular. Such phrase-statements facilitate exact expression, which can be difficult with conventional sentence construction.

Example of No. 5, summary leads:
> SITKA, ALASKA (UPI) — A passenger wrenched his back, a baby swallowed too much salt water, and the pilot suffered a sprained ankle. That was the extent of injuries yesterday when a chartered DC-7 with 103 persons aboard ditched in the Pacific Ocean about 17 miles from here.

Comment: Try this one when you have trouble covering a lot of ground in a hurry. With straight declarative construction, it may take several paragraphs to do this; and such construction tends to bury your highlights, as illustrated by the following technique.

Example of No. 6, upside-down summary leads:
> Machine tool business is looking up.
> Distributors intend to get more sophisticated in their marketing efforts.
> Revisions in tax depreciation laws and the 7 per cent tax credit will help equipment sales.
> Those conclusions accounted for most of the optimism at the AMTDA meeting in Detroit last week.

Comment: A typical summary would bury those key points in this manner:

Three reasons for optimism came out of the AMTDA meeting in Detroit last week: machine tool business is looking up, distributors intend to get more sophisticated in their marketing efforts, and revisions in tax depreciation laws and the 7 per cent tax credit will help sell equipment.

With the recommended technique, the lead, in effect, is turned upside down; and key elements are stated separately.

Note that by putting the key elements out front, statement of the lead is speeded up.

Example of No. 7, promise-of-benefit leads:
> "For thousands who suffer from mystifying attacks of shoulder and back pain along with neck aches, headaches, and undue fatigue, relief is in sight."

Comment: Show biz again. But that's only one consideration. More important, these techniques add to the writer's options for tackling a given situation.

Example of No. 8, prediction leads:
> WASHINGTON (AP) — The President will ask Congress to increase taxes across the board when it reconvenes next week.

Comment: Say you are doing an article on prospects for tax increases and encounter trouble formulating a lead. You discover that you aren't certain what the President will do. This suggests a strategy: take inventory. Write up all the pro's, then the con's, to see how they add up. In doing this, you see — for the first time — that an across-the-board increase is inevitable. Now, how to put this in a lead that's convincing? Using your inventory is one approach; but that's too slow; and the lead is at the end rather than the beginning. In this situation, the prediction lead solves your problem. In terms of credibility, you'd have a more powerful statement if you had an authority say it for you. Still, you are on pretty safe ground. There's a fascination for prediction that works in your favor. Keep in mind, however, that your documentation must support your case in a convincing manner.

Example of No. 9, interpretive leads:

WASHINGTON (AP) — Insiders on Capitol Hill say the President is dropping hints about asking Congress to hike taxes across the board solely for the purpose of getting a show of hands. If the opposition is formidable, he'll back down; if it's lukewarm, he'll reconsider; if there's no reaction, he'll seek public support by claiming that Congress is indifferent about fighting inflation.

Comment: Say you run into a variation of the preceding situation where your pro's and con's aren't so clear-cut; but in thinking about your evidence, it occurs to you that there is an attractive alternative to making a prediction. You suddenly see the President's strategy, or his possible strategy. Do an interpretive lead that enables you to touch all the bases in a hurry. The reader expects you to be logical. But he won't hold you strictly accountable for your interpretation, as long as your slant is plausible. Interpretation, like the summary, enables you to condense the gist of what you have to say in a paragraph or two.

Example of No. 10, straight-quotation leads:

"ServiceCenter prices can't get any lower, and I don't see much of a chance for an increase in the near future," declares Fred James, president of ServiceCenter Inc.

Comment: You gain credibility anytime you put something in quotes. In this situation, the quote is much more convincing than an anonymous third person declarative statement of the same thing. Quotes also solve another type of problem. Suppose you want to say something in your lead that sounds presumptuous or preachy in the third person declarative. You are home free if you can attribute the words to someone else, as illustrated by the next example, which is from *Time.*

Example of No. 11, famous-quotation leads:
Cite famous quotation first:
"He left a Corsair's name to other times,
Link'd with one virtue and a thousand crimes."
— Byron.

Follow with your lead:
Instead of a 19th-century pirate, Byron could have been describing the present federal tax system.

Comment: A heavy statement that may make you feel uncomfortable if "you" are doing the talking in the straight third person. In this instance, you get two bonuses beyond the quotation device per se. You gain the added authority of a famous name. You also pick up an analogy (piracy) from the quote, which helps you characterize your message in a single word. The latter point suggests another insight into why constant emphasis is being put on use of the fewest possible words in your lead. Recall the upside-down summary? Conventional sentence construction always tends to bury or at least blur the message. Take advantage of any device that helps you put your lead in the smallest possible word package. In this instance, the combination of the quote from Byron and the analogy to piracy taken from it enabled the writer to capsulize his message.

Example of No. 12, cliché leads:
In this instance, we draw still another example from *Time*. Cliché first:
"Hell hath no fury like a woman scorned."

Lead next:
According to Gene Schoonmaker, 34, the old saying is an understatement. Consider his plight . . .

Comment: Same basic advantages as the famous quote. You gain the authority of familiarity; and you are able to say a lot in a hurry. There's also a danger. Clichés are crutches. They discourage creativity. By compromising with a cliché, you may be passing up an original that would surface if you worked a little harder. There is no substitute for originality; and it isn't as difficult as many writers make it out to be. For example, if you can't resist a cliché, why not put a new twist on it. For example, "Heaven hath no charm like a woman unscorned," as a variation of the above. Or "Hell hath no fear for a man who hath a woman scorned."

Example of No. 13, play-up-the-urgency leads:
   Now is the time to make preparations to sow seeds in early August.

Comment: Another problem-solver. Say you have a situation that clearly calls for prompt action. But you sense a danger of being over-aggressive. A light touch is desirable. In this instance, the "now is the time" device states the message with minimum acting.

Example of No. 14, challenge-the-reader leads:
   I dare you to match your accounting machine against mine.

Comment: Say you have a situation in which your objective is to get the reader to compare "X" and "Y." Conventionally, you'd come up with two laundry lists: advantages and disadvantages of "X" and advantages and disadvantages of "Y." The ideal would be to have the reader sit back and listen to both sides of the case before you conclude: "Obviously, Y has it." You can bypass the lengthy process with this psychological device. By challenging the reader, you get him involved. This makes it easier for you to state your case. The following technique is closely related.

Example of No. 15, getting-the-reader-involved leads:
   What do you do when you arrive, simultaneously, with three other cars at a four-way boulevard stop?

Comment: You've put the reader in a positon where he "sees" your point himself; you don't have to sell him.

Example of No. 16, "you" leads:
   "You can cut the cost of making tensile specimens by machining them on a production basis, rather than turning them out as you need them."

Comment: A minor psychological device: talking directly to the reader. In some cases, the shift from third person also helps the writer relax. In effect, he is talking to readers.

Example of No. 17, incident or case-history leads:
   SEATTLE, WASH. (UPI) — A blind man took out a hunting license here yesterday.
   In an effort to point out an inadequacy of Washington's hunting laws, Arnold Sadler, a Seattle attorney, and his

Seeing-Eye dog, Heidi, appeared at a downtown hardware store and purchased a hunting license without a hitch.

There is no restriction on vision as far as obtaining a hunting license is concerned in this state.

Sadler does not intend to go hunting.

Comment: Takes more time than any other lead technique, but it is perhaps the most powerful and most underused type among those discussed. The fact that the incident or case history tells a story — something few can resist — is only part of the plus. More important, the device provides a blueprint for telling in a convincing and often dramatic fashion. Good incidents or case histories are typically easier to write than most other leads. In fact, they also provide an ideal way to cover points in documentation.

Where We Go From Here

Leads are a step closer to the promised land. But several more roads must be traveled before we reach our destination.

In fact, it's desirable to take a short backward step before moving ahead to techniques other than leads that enhance our capacity to tell.

Chapter 12

When There Aren't Any Ready-Made Outlines

"Lee would not tell this story, except perhaps to say, 'It was a good trip.' He is not an abstractor, a summarizer. . . . John would tell the entire story this way: 'On a winter trip to Cranesville swamp in search of the northern water shrew (*Sorex palustris*), Bill, Lee and the writer had the happy experience of observing several minks at play in the snow.' . . . There remains my way. I am forever seeking the general significance of such things as shrews and minks and frozen swamps. . . . John is a senior research scientist at a well-known university . . . Lee is an engineer in charge of technical services of a trade association." (Source: "Minks, Shrews, and Men in a Winter Swamp," by Bil Gilbert, *Sports Illustrated.*)

That excerpted lead pinpoints what typically happens when by-the-numbers writers do not have the example of ready-made outlines to fall back on. The negative influences are still at work. Precedent encourages the writer to concentrate on quantities and bare facts.

In the realm of ideas and qualities, the writer's vision is typically confined to interpretations of the obvious and a spate of generalities, truisms, clichés, and jargon that give the reader only part of the message — the nonoriginal and least worthwhile part, at that. The net result: the reader gets only the obvious, literal, shallow, and nonoriginal aspects of a subject or theme.

Implicitly, the writer is not called upon to use all of his intelligence, his creative thinking, his common sense, his judgment, his know-how, his experience. His critical judgment is limited to: "Did I follow precedent?" He is not under any obligation to wonder, "Will this be new and worthwhile and interesting to the reader?"

There is hope here too.

It starts by recognizing the difference between telling about and telling. Or if you prefer, the differences between being general and being explicit.

For the record, both the scientist and the engineer in the case-history lead at the beginning of this chapter were guilty of telling about.

Telling, you'll discover, is largely a matter of how we think as writers. The aim, as usual, is to provide the reader with maximum content.

Chapter 13

Telling Versus Telling About

A writer settled for this generalization, "Open hearth furnaces require quantities of bricks."

He was asked, "Can you be more explicit than quantities?"

"Tons?" he offered.

"Closer, but try again," he was urged.

Ultimately, he came up with, "Open hearth furnaces require several boxcar loads of bricks."

Not perfection, but far better than "quantities."

One clue: you can begin to visualize "boxcar loads," but "quantities" is a nonentity.

Another writer came up with, "The stock market is weak because of the international situation."

"Weak" is jargon, a handy generalization that relieves the writer of his responsibility to think.

"International situation" is also a generality.

A discerning reader would ask:

"What do you mean by weak?"

"Which international situation do you refer to?"

There's a point here: anytime you raise a question — directly or indirectly — and leave it unanswered, you are telling about, rather than telling.

The net result: you are withholding information the reader should have.

In the last example, the writer was quizzed.

"Weak," it turned out, meant "The average price of industrial stocks on the New York Stock Exchange dropped $1 under yesterday's high of $147."

Why? (international situation):

". . . when Premier Khrushchev threatened to send troops into Bessarabia."

Remember, the writer, not the reader, should be asking the questions.

Unfortunately, generalization — telling about — has the sanction of widespread practice. It looks right and sounds right because everyone else does it.

Let's look at another example — a verbatim account (from *Aviation Week*) of weightlessness in space flight as described by one of this nation's first astronauts. Italics flag telling-about symptoms.

> "It was a *pretty fascinating phenomenon.* The view out of the window was *unbelievable.* You can't take your eyes away from that window [for] the first few seconds of weightless flying. It's *incredible. There aren't enough words in the English language to describe the beauty.* I felt this during the last part of powered flight. I was supposed to monitor the inertial guidance system's performance, *but it's really a chore* to get your . . . as soon as the spacecraft pitches over and you ride on the horizon . . . *you can't* . . . it's just a tremendous effort to get your head back in the cockpit and look at those instruments. *I think it's the sort of thing that one is really fortunate to get to be able to do. I was impressed.*"

About Spaghetti and Other Matters

Next time you write "spaghetti," ask yourself, "What kind?"
Stelline?
It looks like a little star with a hole in the middle.
Ditali?
It looks like a short piece of macaroni.
Mafalde?
It looks like a long noodle with edges crimped on each side.
Fusilli?
It looks like a long noodle with kinks in it.
Gnocchi?

It looks like a little oyster shell.
Farfalle?
It looks like a little bow tie.
Rotelle?
It looks like a spring.
Or how about ofe, or maruzzelle, or fettucine, or cappelletti, or oochi, or di lupo, or cavetelli, or emgelli, or rigatoni, or taingoli?
There are at least 17 specific types of spaghetti.
Spaghetti is a telling-about word, a generalization.
Only exact words tell.
Don't settle for tree. Say birch or oak or poplar.
Don't say dog. Say poodle or beagle or German shepherd.
Don't say railway car. Say boxcar or flatcar or gondola.
You must assume that the reader knows gnocchi and fettucine and white birches and ball peen hammers.
When things have exact names, use them.
The same applies to numbers.
Don't say several when you mean seven.
You can apply the technique by converting a generality to a number. Compare a "significant" saving with a "50%" saving.
The latter is much more explicit than the former.
It's also possible that you may want to go beyond "50%" to spell out why it is "significant."
Here's what a *Newsweek* writer did to make $40-million, the cost of making the movie "Cleopatra" more meaningful (explicit).
He wrote, "It is more than half the endowment of Princeton University. It exceeds the total expenditures of the United States Government during George Washington's administration. It is eighteen times the recent selling price of Rembrandt's 'Aristotle Contemplating the Bust of Homer.' "
In that case, comparison was the telling device.
It's also possible to make qualities explicit with numbers. A writer for *Life,* for example, took the following tack to express the "vastness" of the movie "How the West Was Won."
He used exact numbers: "With 1,200 buffaloes, 875 horses, 350 Indians, 24 stars, a cast of 12,617 players, and every trick in the horse-opera repertory, M-G-M's How the West Was Won is not the best western ever made, but it surely is the biggest and gaudiest."
Writers look for comparisons, likenesses, differences. Particularly

when they want to go beyond the facts, numbers, and exact things. A number of devices are available.

Similes & Such

Say you want to do better than "He ran fast."

How about "He ran like a barefoot boy on a hot tar road."

A simile, a form of comparison, is usually accompanied by "like" or "as."

In building similes, avoid clichés. They're usable, but always try the do-it-yourself route first. Concentrate on everyday things, instead of the ancient or literary.

For example, to express "beaten up," how about "as out of shape as a toothpaste tube shared by six small children."

For example, to express "unsalvageable," how about "as useless as a second-hand Kleenex."

For example, to express "uniqueness," how about "as different as a Michelob bottle."

For example, to express "misplaced humor," how about "as funny as a flat tire in an expressway traffic jam."

For example, to express "universality," how about "as common as a TV antenna."

For example, to express "neatness," how about "He always looks like he just had a haircut."

For example, to express "falseness," how about "She is as phony as a plastic orchid."

After Similes, Metaphors

"He is built like a bulldozer" is a simile.

Remove "built like" and you have a metaphor.

"He is a bulldozer."

Note what happens. A metaphor changes the name of a person or thing. Such devices give you another dimension in expression or, to be more particular, allow you to become more exact or explicit than the original or common name.

To put it another way, the devices we're talking about help us to exceed the normal, often single, point of view.

Devices that focus our attention on understatement or overstatement, for example, encourage us to look for contradictions, inconsistencies, paradoxes, ironies. Incidents force us to look for little stories or case histories that make a point or convey a message in a dramatic or convincing manner.

The objective is to open up a whole new world; one in which we think about and see the total of our information as writers.

At the same time, there are pitfalls in reaching out beyond the humdrum. For one thing, judgment is required.

Obscurity is a danger, for example.

To get back to metaphors, say we write: "He's another Clyde McCoy."

The writer must realize that the comparison will be lost on popular-music buffs who weren't around in the thirties and forties.

This suggests that in the case of similes and metaphors, where the writer is creating content, he should play it safe by sticking with the familiar. Such as everyday things ("as noisy as a chainsaw," for example); or current things ("as well-known as the Watergate principals," for example).

Among current things, take advantage of this season's popular songs and plays, this season's political climate, heroes, and goats; this season's fads in women's and men's clothing and hair styles; this season's hot topics in sciences; and so on.

More Telling Techniques

Onomatopoeia is the esoteric name for a specialized form of word coinage. You name a thing for a sound or some other aspect or quality clearly associated with it.

Example: "Bang-bang" for cowboy movie.

Synecdoche is another-change-of-name device.

Example: "Wheels" for "auto."

In this instance, the name of a part or major characteristic becomes the name of the whole.

Start with "It was a gathering of men with great minds."

You convert that to a synecdoche by converting that to "It was a gathering of great minds."

One more:

Change "20 infantrymen" to "20 rifles."

For hairsplitters, the last two examples are officially called *metonymy*. But it and synecdoche are so close there's no reason to haggle over which is which.

Another device, *antonomasia,* boils down to "calling instead." It's generally applied where there is an alternative name: "his grace" for a member of nobility; "Mr. Show Biz" for a famous actor; "his honor" for a judge.

Personification permits the writer to give life to a thing or an abstraction, as in "No other gasoline can make this claim."

"Gasoline" can't do anything of the sort; but with due care, personification is a useful device.

A device with the strange name of *oxymoron* suggests that there are times when we can combine two contradictory terms to advantage.

Example:

"He's a cheerful pessimist."

Or:

"It was a sharp-dull remark."

Euphemism is characterized by the cliché "damning with faint praise." It's a polite or watered-down way of being critical or stating the unpleasant.

Example:

"I've seen worse examples."

The opposite, plain talk, is called *dysphemism.*

Litotes — stating the affirmative negatively — is an offshoot of euphemism.

Example:

"He made not a few mistakes."

Hyperbole is overstatement.

Example, from *Time's* movie section:

"She plays . . . a woman with the brain of a flea, the heart of a whale, the tongue of a toad, the devotion of a dog, the cunning of a serpent, and the innocence of a noisy old parrot."

Meiosis is the opposite: understatement.

Example:

"He was scarcely bigger than a golf bag."

Punning and *word coinage* may be lumped together. Both require discretion. Both devices — and others — are combined in the following example from *Time:*

". . . Jim Hutton, 26, is an unpolished bean pole (6 feet 3 inches) who gangles at all angles like a second string center on a YMCA basketball squad, but sputters sourprises like a bright, green Lemmon. (Jack, that is.)"

Always be on the alert for opportunities to play on words or ideas.

Take a statement like "The threat of warfare is barking close at the heels of security."

"Barking" suggests a refinement.

How about:

"The wolf of warfare is snarling close at the heels of American security." (Note: alliteration, "wolf of warfare" in this sentence, is OK in small doses.)

Another example: "Is your sales pitch out of tune? It is if you are talking too much and listening too little."

"Pitch" suggests a music analogy.

How about:

"Is your sales pitch out of tune? It is if you are singing too much and listening too little."

In *a priori* reasoning we go from cause to effect.

The reverse (effect to cause) is called *a fortiori* reasoning.

The former is common, for example, in conventional sentence construction, such as "He pulled the trigger and the gun went bang."

The latter, being less conventional, may be used as a change of pace in sentence construction, such as "Bang went the gun after he pulled the trigger."

Repetition of a word or phrase is called *anaphora*.

Example:

"He bowed, he fell, he passed out."

You can get another effect when succeeding sentences have parallel construction (such as the last example) and you reverse the order of the second one.

Start with "I can't afford to buy it; I am obliged to make it."

Convert that to "I can't afford to buy it; to make it I am obliged."

Variety can also be obtained with a surprise break in natural sequence, called *anacoluthon*.

Example:

"Here they come down the home stretch. Wow! He tripped."

You can get emphasis with contrasting phrases or sentences (*antithesis*).

Example:

"Hot was his head; cold was his heart."

Syllepsis gives us a different way of telling by what amounts to combining conventional and unconventional applications of a word.

For example, you can "lean" on a desk but not an abstraction like a joke.

Example of syllepsis:

"He leaned heavily on his desk and stale jokes."

Anastrophe describes a reversal in conventional word order, such as "came the dawn" instead of "the dawn came."

The straight third person (this style) is the dullest possible way of telling in large doses. There seems to be an allergy to second- or first-person construction.

"You" construction seems to encourage writers to explain, amplify, be explicit. It can also destarch stiff-collar writers. Writing down should be guarded against, also any tendencies toward pedantry and undue length.

"I" construction scares the pants off most writers. They are super-self-critical because "I" am talking. Once shyness wears off, there's a clear and present danger of becoming a bore.

Another aspect of sentence construction is pertinent.

Conventional construction normally puts secondary information up front and pushes the primary to the rear. A burying influence results.

A conventional sentence:

"The governor of Ohio today announced a $1-billion tax cut for industry."

By turning this around, you put the meat up front:

"A $1-billion tax cut for industry was announced today by the governor of Ohio."

The technique is particularly handy in writing leads. You want to do all you can to get off to a fast start in your first sentence.

Another device, dialog, is particularly suitable for documentation. Study how it is used by writers of articles on popular subjects and fiction.

One other point: all the devices discussed in this chapter should be applied in all elements: titles, leads, and documentation.

A Preliminary Summing Up

This completes our analysis of the impact of ready-made outlines on content.

Other aspects of by-the-numbers writing, which also have negative influences on content and "how" we write, will be the next subject.

Chapter 14

Another View of the By-The-Numbers World

There are five standards for by-the-numbers writing practices that compound the undesirable influences of ready-made outlines:

1. Standards that encourage improper personification.

Preliminary comment: This literature is supposed to be serious and factual; but — strangely — precedent sanctions science fiction (bestowing human qualities on things and abstractions) and inaccuracy (elevating no-facts to the status of facts).

2. Standards that promote a standard language.

Preliminary comment: A language that is limited to blacks and whites. Two results: shades of meaning are out of reach, and a monotonous sameness is produced.

3. Standards that encourage indirect telling.

Preliminary comment: They also promote wordiness and obfuscation.

4. Standards that encourage piling up of modifiers and unconventional word order.

Preliminary comment: The language is clumsy, unnatural, and barely literate.

5. Standards that promote various forms of redundancy.

Preliminary comment: Saying it more than once when repetition isn't necessary to meaning or emphasis causes unnecessary length, adds to the shallowness and literalness of this literature, and compounds its boring sameness and dullness.

In the next five chapters, we'll examine these standards, in reverse order.

Chapter 15

Saying It More Than Once More Than Once

"A custom product manufacturer produces parts . . ."
Comment: "Manufacturer" makes "produces" unnecessary. Both "product" and "parts" aren't needed. "Parts" is more explicit than "product."
Better to write:
"A manufacturer of custom parts . . ."
This example illustrates a common form of redundancy: unnecessary repetition of the same or similar words.
The same practice is apparent where a meaning or an idea is repeated without purpose.
Example: "A custom product manufacturer produces parts to an individual customer's specific needs and specifications."
Comment: Everything following "parts" is excess baggage. It repeats and explains the standard definition of "custom."
Again, better to write:
"A manufacturer of custom parts . . ."
Another example of the same thing:
"A coke research oven simulates plant conditions to produce coke like that from full-sized ovens."
Comment: Check the meaning of "simulates."
Better to write:
"A coke research oven simulates plant conditions."
Another example:
"The plan helps to avoid parochialism and narrowmindedness."

Comment: Either "parochialism" or "narrowmindedness" will do.
Another example:
"The visiting inspector will make a spot-check of his own choice of whatever is on the line at the moment."

Comment: The word "spot-check" *says* "of his own choice of whatever is on the line at the moment"; 13 unnecessary words. The same thing can be said in seven:

"The visiting inspector will spot-check the line."

Diehards will argue, "Big deal! You save a word here and there." They're missing the point. First, we're talking about a discipline: don't use one more word that you need. Second, we're dealing with single sentences in the examples. By concentrating on redundancy alone, it's possible to squeeze down the number of words in a piece of this literature by 25% or more. Not only that, redundancy adds to monotony and drabness.

You'll also encounter redundancy where explanation, definition, interpretation, and conclusions aren't necessary.

Example:
"Rough rule of thumb."

Comment: Adding "rough" to the cliché is as ridiculous as appending "average" to "man in the street." Both are sanctioned by universal usage.

Example:
"The plant operated continuously, around the clock, 24 hours a day."

Comment: That's saying the same thing three times.

Example:
"Disorderly chaos."

Comment: Presumably to set this condition apart from "orderly chaos." "Chaos" does the job on its own. Why insult the reader with inane explanation?

Example:
"Sales in January were $300,000 compared with $200,000 in June, meaning that they increased $100,000 during the period. If the same rate of increase holds in August, sales that month will rise to $400,000."

Comment: There's no reason to go beyond "June" if you haven't anything worthwhile to say. The interpretation and projection are painfully obvious.

You also see redundancy where context makes repetition of a point or fact unnecessary.

Example:
"The company is building a new plant. The new plant will be completed in June. It will cost $2-million."

Comment: Now the detective work must be a little more sophisticated. We're looking beyond what happens inside a single sentence.

This form of redundancy — for want of a better name, we'll call it contextual — accounts for much of the fat in this literature.

For example, once a subject is established, it is typically restated or rephrased in every conceivable way. In an article on welding aluminum, the author said "welding" in one way or another 139 times. "Aluminum" was repeated 67 times. At least 90% of the repetition was pointless. The countermeasure is suggested by a restatement of the example:

"The company is building a $2-million plant that will be completed in June."

Check the original: Note how "new plant" is repeated in the second sentence; then repeated with "it" in the third. Also, "new" isn't necessary. You can't build an "old plant." The exercise suggests taking a look at what is said in all three sentences. It's obvious that everything can be incorporated into one.

Many redundancies are in the form of couplets that seem to be handed down from generation to generation.

Any time you see "imports," for example, you can bet it is preceded by "foreign."

Is there such a thing as a *nonforeign* import?

Surprisingly, you'll find one of the infrequent outbreaks of innovation in this area. The practice seems to be, "If at all possible, find a way to say it more than once." Two examples:

"Foreign imports *from overseas.*"

"Beating swords into plowshares *for peaceful purposes.*"

Guidelines for Redundancy Watchers

The flamboyant Two-Headed Couplet (*Italian* spaghetti, *successful* antidote, *coordinated* teamwork, *close* proximity) is easy to spot and subdue. Other equally exotic species are camouflaged in drab plumage.

Take the supposedly harmless "the." In some habitats, it serves a useful purpose. In others, it is a word waster.

How do you distinguish between the two?

Try the ear test.

Remove the "the," as in the preceding sentence. Reread the sentence. Does it sound natural without it? In this instance, "Try ear test," is offensive telegraphese. Leave "the" in.

How about:

"The polish is added."

In this application, "polish is added" sounds a little more polished than "the polish is added." In fact, where succeeding sentences are involved, removal of an excess "the" can add polish to the transition. The practice is as desirable as the replacement of tack words.

Hunting and eradicating "the's" has the appearance of a minor sport, yet you'll be surprised by their abundance. In fact, go to the first word in this paragraph. "The" would normally precede "hunting." It was intentionally avoided in this instance. The result? The sentence is a little classier without it — although this one would't be. However, you can remove the "the" before "result" in the preceding sentence and "the" before "the" in this one. Notice that removable "the's" can start a sentence, or be located inside one.

Another "the" matter, though not related to redundancy, is pertinent to the general discussion. Starting a number of succeeding sentences with "the" reflects an obvious lack of feel for language. However, there is a tendency to overapply the role.

Some beadstringers object to starting successive paragraphs with "the" even though they may be separated by several sentences. Their remedy can result in a strained application of a substitute for the second "the." In such cases, remind them: "Look at the last word in the preceding paragraph; if it isn't "the," it's OK to start the next paragraph with "the." The one at the beginning of the first paragraph is too far removed from the beginning of the second paragraph to do any harm — unless the first paragraph contains only one sentence.

Back to other forms of redundancy. Be wary of:

Standard words and phrases.

Combinations of the general and specific.

Needless repetition of words and ideas.

Just plain wordiness.

Gratuitous explanation or qualification.

Two sentences (or more) that do the work of one.

Standard Words and Phrases

How often do you see the following?
"for a period of three to four hours."
Drop "a period of."
"in their respective areas."
"Respective" doesn't add anything.
"in order to."
"To" can do it alone.
"before the October 1 price increase goes into effect."
Eliminate the last three words.
"rubber-type tire."
Drop "type."
"since they were first introduced."
"First" isn't needed.
"offers its services where needed."
Stop at "services."
"used in applications."
"Used" says it.
"company-by-company basis."
"Basis" is a standard, and redundant.

In some instances, more than elimination is required. Ask: "What's a shorter way of saying this?"

Example:
"In the near future."
How about "soon."

Example:
"within the realm of possibility."
You can say the same thing with "possible."

Example:
"Tests were conducted on the behalf of AIME."
Try: "Tests were for AIME."

General-Specific Combinations

Example:
"A small, two-ounce can."
"Drop 'small'." If you have the specific, don't use the general too.

Example:
"The tool cuts cleanly, without distortion or burring."

In this case "cleanly" is general; "without distortion or burring" is specific. Eliminate "cleanly."

Example:

"Precision cutting of heavy gage sheet metal is done by this machine. It cuts stainless steel up to 10 gage and nonferrous metals up to 8 gage."

In this instance, the first sentence is general; the second, specific. Better to combine the two sentences into one:

"This machine precision cuts stainless steel up to 10 gage and nonferrous metals up to 8 gage."

Needless Repetition of Words and Ideas

Example:

"They believe that for the most part it was generally overlooked."

Note the repetition of an idea. "For the most part" and "generally" are one and the same. How about: "They believe it was generally overlooked."

Example:

"He believes that it is the only means to eliminate polio and its paralyzing effects for all time."

If polio is eliminated, so are "its paralyzing effects for all time." Nine times out of ten, you should stop at "eliminated." There's nothing wrong about intentionally repeating for emphasis; however, such a noble motive is not common. Remember the rule: Don't use one more word than you need.

Example:

"He's optimistic about prospects for sales."

You double up with both "optimistic" and "prospects." Drop "prospects for" in this instance.

Just Plain Wordiness

Wordiness makes this literature pompous. Anytime you run into doubletalk or gobbledegook, it's a pretty good sign that the writer hasn't figured out what he's trying to say and is thrashing about. Writing long is always easier than writing short.

Example:

"Output has continued strong in the face of difficulties stemming from adverse weather conditions."

How about:

"Output has continued strong despite bad weather." Seven words instead of 14.

Analyze the following. Look for shortcuts:

"A $2-million program to increase the production capacity of the only steel mill in Puerto Rico is under way. Capacity of Jose Frito Inc. will be boosted 50%. The specialty mill makes reinforcing bars for the island's booming construction business."

Here's a shorter route:

"A $2-million program to hike the capacity of Puerto Rico's only steel mill 50% is under way. The specialty mill, Jose Frito Inc., makes reinforcing bars for the island's booming construction business."

Result: a saving of eight words.

Example:

"Other measures suggested as ways the railroad industry can help itself include . . ."

Ask: What's the idea behind "ways the railroad industry can help itself?"

Answer: "self-help."

Try this approach:

"Other self-help measures for the railroad industry include . . ."

Gratuitous Explanation or Qualification

This is an annoying practice that compounds the shallowness and dullness of this literature.

Example:

After stating, "Two nonsupervisory members of the staff are chosen — in alphabetical order — to sit in on daily staff meetings for one week," the writer added, "when every one of the nonsupervisors has had a chance to attend meetings for a week and state his views, the order begins all over again."

The writer intended to explain what happens when everyone has had his turn. That's implicit in the first sentence. However, if there's any fear of ambiguity, it would be easy enough to rephrase the statements:

"Two nonsupervisory members of the staff, chosen in alphabetical order, sit in on daily staff meetings for one week. The process is repeated when the last two have had their turns."

Example:

"The book, if learned, will help the foreigner get along in Russia."

Think about it: "if learned" is an insult to the reader.
Example:
"When completed the plant will produce bread at a rate of 4000 to 6000 loaves an hour."

Some background is necessary here. The writer had already established that the plant — designed to bake bread exclusively — was under construction. Under the circumstances, "when completed" and "bread" aren't necessary. Also, "at the rate of" is a standard phrase to be avoided.

A suggested rewrite:
"The plant will produce 4000 to 6000 loaves an hour."

Two Sentences (or More) That Do the Work of One

Example:
"Highway mesh has been moving slowly in New England this year. The same is true of building mesh."

A possible alternative:
"Highway and building mesh have been moving slowly in New England this year."

Example:
"The company will buy equipment for its Windsor plant. The used machinery will be used to make component parts."

A possible alternative:
"The company will buy used parts-making equipment for its Windsor plant."

Note "component parts." It's an example of a Two-Headed Couplet. Either "component" or "parts" will do.

Genuine Two-Headed Couplets

The following examples of Two-Headed Couplets are presented at the risk of boredom to impress you with their ubiquity. Italics indicate the offenders.

Present incumbent	*Informed* market authority
*Pre*plan	Allow freedom for *future* expansion
Currently pending	In *current* vogue
Temporary expedient	*A few* scattered increases
Past history	Follows fads *up and down*
Factually correct	Lack of *enough* orders

Premiered its *new* car
The need for better coordination *and* liaison
He was extremely candid *in his convictions*
Light gray in *color*
We need cheaper Space Age materials *at less cost*
It has been the subject of speculation *and conjecture*
Regaining *lost* confidence
Expatriated *back to his native land*
Frustrating dilemma
Distorted *out of shape*
Legislation pending *now*
Some slight evidence
Farfetched, impractical pipedream
Current status
Plan *ahead*
Specifically earmarked
Temporary stopgap
Past record
Combined pooling of resources
Brief résumé
Anticipate greater success *in the future*
Leading expert
Bonanza of *valuable* information

Completely eliminated
Lack of business *in sufficient volume*
Orders are limping along *at a snail's pace*
Meet *together*
It *still* remains with us
About on the verge
Reverts *back*
Camaraderie and *team spirit*
Baseless rumors
Lint *particles*
Bellwether *sign*
The month of June
Behind a veil of *strict* secrecy
Invisible *to the naked eye*
Forward planning
Consensus *of opinion*
Specific example
Actual photograph
Past experience
Uses *and applications*
Business recession
Inside closeup
Used as a fulcrum *for leverage*
Historical retrospection
Small inkling
Good common sense
Rule-of-thumb *guideline*
General, across-the-board price increase

Chapter 16

Piling Them Up and Pennsylvania Dutch

Part of the ritual of technical writing is a ground rule that adjectives have emotional overtones foreign to science and engineering. If the truth were known, a run-of-the-mill technical writer outdoes Charles Dickens any day of the week. Typically, adjectives are stacked so high you are lucky if you can find the noun — or have the patience to look for it.

Monsters like this are common:

"Here is a new, 900 ton, 1200 hp, DC, 24 by 44 ft, high speed, numerically controlled, Overman-Underman-type metal cutting tool."

Comment: It doesn't look wrong if everyone else does it that way. It's also obvious the standard does not promote a feel for language or good taste. It can be argued that specifics are being provided. The quarrel is with how they are packaged.

In analyzing the sentence, it's clear that it contains three essential elements: new, Overman-Underman, metal cutting tool.

Working from that base, the next consideration is: How to dispose of some of the adjectives in the first sentence; then come up with a way to accommodate the remainder?

One possibility:

"Here is a new, numerically controlled, Overman-Underman metal cutting tool. This high speed, 900 ton unit operates on direct current, is powered by a 1200 hp motor, and measures 24 by 44 ft."

Version No. 2 boosts the word count; but there is justification. The alternative is a hard-to-read, barely literate form of expression.

Punctuation buffs may point out several opportunities to join compound adjectives with hyphens. Again, an alternative must be considered: with the hyphens you have a daisy chain of words that resembles German more than English.

At best, constructions that pile up adjectives are clumsy, unnatural, and barely literate.

A related practice gets a similar result.

Take such constructions as:

"U. S. firms' business proposals."

The natural construction is:

"Business proposals of U. S. firms."

An apostrophe and a clumsy genitive construction are traded for an "of." These constructions can be so obtuse as to require translation.

Such a lack of feeling for language provides a rationalization for unchallenged Pennsylvania Dutch constructions reminiscent of "I'll throw mother from the train a kiss."

Example:

"It sells to industry heavy water."

Precedent to the contrary, the natural construction is:

"It sells heavy water to industry."

Technically, the problem is one of syntax — word order.

Chapter 17

Circuitous Telling

"The additive functions by dispersing sludge in the form of small particles."

A by-the-numbers writer wouldn't see anything wrong with the above, because it has the sanction of widespread usage.

Problem: the message is stated in a bassackward fashion.

It's the long way of telling.

More words than needed are used.

Remedy: Use a direct, rather than an indirect, route:

"The additive disperses sludge as small particles."

Example:

"The method is successful in joining dissimilar metals."

Better:

"The method joins dissimilar metals."

Comment: A specific in place of "the method" is better practice.

Such as:

"Dissimilar metals can be inertia welded."

Also note the personification: "the method is successful." This is a common misapplication of the technique.

Another example of indirect telling:

"Tungsten plating of a metal can be accomplished with vapor phase techniques."

Better:

"You can plate tungsten with vapor phase techniques."

Example:

"Boration was effected in water."

Better:

"We dissolved borax."

Such statements as "boration was effected in water" have the qualities of a strange foreign language. The reader must translate. At the least, indirectness promotes wordiness.

Compare:

"One of our prime objectives will continue to be to effect needed price restorations."

With this translation:

"Higher prices are needed."

Compare:

"Purchasing agents are not achieving their full potential in helping the earnings positions of their companies."

With this translation:

"Purchasing agents can do more to help their companies improve earnings."

A strange language.

A construction that promotes prolixity.

Technically, here's how indirectness is explained: The object of the verb in the active voice becomes the subject in the passive. Typically, two verb forms appear in passive construction.

Chapter 18

A Rubber-Stamp Language

In an Associated Press feature "Is French Language on the Way Out?" writer James Bacon reported that Frank Sinatra has a standard noun, "Clyde," that takes care of many of his communication needs.

Frank comments on restaurant to waiter, "Nice Clyde you got here."

Frank orders more wine, "Give me some more of that Clyde."

Frank asks for his hat, "Get me my Clyde with the white band on it."

Frank gets into his car (Clyde) and drives off.

A by-the-numbers writer has a kit of "Clydes." Some are nouns. Many are verbs and adjectives. A thesaurus isn't needed. There's a standard word for every occasion.

You always "conduct" a study, survey, course, sales campaign, or what have you. You always say "available" supplies, know-how, facts, tonnage, or what have you. You always "successfully" weld, paint, pass a test, close a contract, or what have you.

It's a monotonous, rubber-stamp language.

Any time you have the need to express the idea "increase," for example, you use it without regard to its suitability or repetition.

In this shortened example, a writer "increased" ten times in two pages of copy:

"Applications are *increasing* for two reasons . . . use in aerospace units is *increasing* . . . spindle size was *increased* . . . we *increased* production . . . the move enables the firm to *increase* spindle speed . . . rates have been *increased* from 250 to 4000 per hour . . . ABC Company sees *increasing* demand . . . XYZ Corporation notes *increasing* interest in . . . it *increases* productivity . . . it *increased* interest in the drive . . .''

Synonyms provide relief, but that isn't getting to the source of the problem.

Standard words only approximate what we should be saying.

They are a poor compromise for the exact word.

With standard language, you settle for:

"increased power and increased feed rates."

After consideration — a practice not encouraged by standard language — you find you can come closer with something like:

"more power and higher feed rates."

In some instances, the standard may be the wrong word.

Example:

A government official commented on a chronic shortage of railway freight cars. The problem stemmed from an industry practice: a railroad company will often lease cars to meet unexpected surges in demand, as an alternative to building, which would add to the total available in the industry.

The official resorted to a standard word, "inadequate," to characterize the problem.

He said the shortage was "due to inadequate ownership." But quality of ownership is not at issue.

"Lack of ownership" is closer to the truth.

Again, such problems can't be solved with word jockeying.

We think with words; and the standards being contested encourage writers to think in black and white only. There are no colors. There are no in-between shades. There are no nuances or shades of meaning.

A by-the-numbers writer will report:

"Sales increased 0.001 per cent,"

Or "Sales increased 100 per cent."

It does not occur to him that:

"Sales inched up 0.001 per cent."

Or that "Sales soared 100 per cent."

Tip: If a word or group of words looks right or sounds right, stop. You've probably flushed a standard word or phrase.

Don't bother looking for a synonym.

Take another think at what you have to say.

Don't settle for less than the exact word.

Don't pass up opportunities to use colors and in-between shades.

Chapter 19

Science Fiction and No-Facts

In the proper place, it is convenient to bestow human qualities on inanimate things.

We all know, for example, that a corporation is a thing that exists only on paper; yet no one objects or is confused when we give it power of speech—as in "ABC Corporation said today."

Communication would be cumbersome if we had to spin out all the interrelationships avoided by that shorthand.

We'd have to say something like:

"John Jones, on authority of the board of directors [a fiction] of ABC Corporation [a fiction created in the state of Delaware, also a fiction], said today."

It's also convenient for advertising copywriters to personify products so they can boast, "Brand X is the only gasoline that will pay your towing bill if your car does not start this winter."

However, there is no excuse for personification as a regular way of thinking.

The practice is constantly overused and misused.

A writer can't help but be a little less than logical when he writes:

"We think these gears could have meaning for race cars."

Or: "Stainless steel fears new wheels."

Or: "It is good policy, therefore, for a product of long standing to turn and look backward for 10 to 20 years or longer, as a measure of progress and as an aid in planning for the future."

Or: "Many current training programs, in their attempt to cover a little bit of everything, run the risk of impressing the new employee with the thought that he needs to be a generalist to survive."

Pure unadulterated horsefeathers.

The only way to untilt such thinking is to make people the agents of action.

Instead of "Stainless steel fears new wheels," what is involved is:

"People who make and sell stainless steel wheels fear competition from another group of people who make wheels from different materials."

Likewise, "It is good policy for people who make a product of long standing to turn and look backward . . ."

Likewise, "Many framers of training programs, in their attempt to cover a little bit of everything, run the risk of scaring new employees . . ."

The practice is even more objectionable on the next plateau.

Fictions and nothings become superbeings with superstatus.

Presumably, people have no control or authority over them.

Witness:

A company (a fiction) announces: "Prices threaten to go up if the union wins its demands."

Implicitly, people in the company have no control over a nothing called prices.

Prices go up and down at will.

Or they respond automatically to a given set of conditions.

In the same vein, you see:

"Inventories will continue to build up."

Presumably on their own.

This is a form of doublethink.

In the same category is the learned nonsense dished up by learned experts.

They can defend or prosecute any case with super-no-things subject only to the flexible laws of science fiction.

Witness:

"Prices will automatically move up because of two things: product quality has improved, and the cost of the materials in the products has gone up."

More horsefeathers.

In the much more sophisticated world of reality, people in companies raise and lower prices in response to a variety of factors and circumstances, not to mention whim, hunch, guts, and greed.

Conceivably, competition can force prices down at a time when costs and quality are headed in the opposite direction.

Such thinking helps to explain the obfuscation in this literature.

That's not the last trick, however.

The seas of reality are further riled by a related practice.

Call it factmaking.

It's January. Employment statistics for November of the previous year have just been released by the government. They are the latest available numbers.

A business writer or economist analyzes the statistics and reports in January:

"According to government statistics, employment is uptrending."

Unsuspecting readers think the writer is talking about "now," January. The writer elevates a November fact to a January fact. His reporting license does not extend beyond, "Employment was uptrending last November. Statistics for January are not available."

Both the writer and the government won't know what the January situation will be until March, two months hence.

These distinctions are ignored.

The apogee in factmaking is reached when a writer gives factlike status to a premise and spins off a series of conclusions from it.

Example:

An authority speaking to an international conference in Rome used the following fiction-fact for his premise:

"Scientific management is the touchstone that can bring great benefits to the underdeveloped nations of the world."

Armed with a 400-horsepower panacea, he proceeded along the route:

"It is evident that without scientific management neither technological progress nor investment of capital can cause the potentially attainable maximum increase in output . . ."

Add more horsefeathers.

The entire speech did not contain one fact or observation from experience.

Yet it sounded like gospel.

Worse still, the deception probably wasn't intentional. The man actually thought he was bringing wisdom to the masses. Certainly, no one would question him. You can find precedent — chapter and verse — in crushing volume.

Chapter 20

Summing Up

It is interesting and instructive to take a quick inventory of what the by-the-numbers writer has going against him.

He relies on standards and practices which encourage him to:

- Create a science-fiction world in which stainless steel fears new wheels and gears have meaning for race cars.
- Give nothings like prices the ability to move about at will.
- Elevate history to now status.
- Convert a premise to a fact.
- Use a language that's limited to black and white.
- Adopt an indirect way of telling that amounts to a strange foreign language that requires translation by the reader and promotes prolixity.
- Pile up modifiers, adding to the cumbersomeness of the language for this literature.
- Place words in contexts that amount to Pennsylvania Dutch.
- Use all manner of redundancies that compound the wordiness and dullness and shallowness of this literature.

In addition, use of ready-made outlines (another practice) encourages the writer to:

- Bury his lead.
- Underdevelop direct documentation of his subject or theme.
- Overdevelop documentation that is collateral to his subject or theme.
- Place great demands on the patience of readers by mixing direct and collateral documentation.
- Confine development to the literal, shallow, and nonoriginal

aspects of a subject or theme even when a ready-made outline is not available.
- Withhold information the reader expects, wants, and deserves.

In total, the writer is not encouraged to utilize his natural resources.

If you put native ability to communicate on a 1-to-10 scale, a typical by-the-numbers writer scores from 7 to 10 in conversation. His rating plummets to the 1-to-3 level when he writes.

A reformed by-the-numbers writer shouldn't encounter more than the normal number of headaches and frustrations inherent in the writing process.

The fundamentals are relatively few in number:
1. What you do before you write is at least equal in importance to the manner in which you put words on paper.
2. Build organization — which is based primarily on how we read — into your outline.
3. The objective is to provide the reader with the most possible worthwhile content.
4. Write two drafts.
5. Edit your second draft.

Those basics apply to essentially all forms of this literature.

Correspondence is not included, because it is a separate art. Use of ready-made outlines is not a common problem here. But standards relating to language practices are just as epidemic in correspondence as they are in this literature.

What You Do Before You Write

Take inventory after gathering your raw materials. You'll have a head start, because the "count" is mental as well as physical. You won't get anyplace until you have a handle on what you have — and what you haven't.

Understanding won't come until your thinking becomes organized, disciplined, meditative.

You will probably have to force the onset of thinking like a writer by use of a technique such as a brainstorming first draft.

When you are raring to start writing (ready psychologically), you should decide first: Do I have something worthwhile to say? Or should I do the poor old reader a favor and abandon the project?

If you decide to go ahead, make a realistic outline based on your inventory. You'll bypass the normal gestation period if you do this before completing your inventory.

Blueprint for Organization

If you use a general-purpose format, here are your basic requirements:
- Lead first, preferably in the first sentence or first paragraph. If you use an incident or case-history lead, make sure you don't bury your subject or theme.
- Primary documentation of lead next, starting immediately after the lead is finished. Carefully select two, or three, or four major points. Stick with them. Develop each in depth.
- Secondary documentation last, if it is justified.
- Stop when you have finished. Don't use one more word than you need.

If you use a special-purpose format, your basic requirements are the same as above, with two exceptions:
- Tailor lead for special-interest reader.
- Tailor documentation for him, too.

Giving the Reader the Most Possible Worthwhile Content

More than anything else, this means being explicit, as opposed to being general.

Tell. Avoiding telling about.

Take advantage of techniques that expand your capacity to tell.

Take advantage of in-house materials, particularly if what you are writing about is based on information generated in your work.

If you have to dig up your own materials, as in speechwriting, put first emphasis on original information. Remember that the people who listen to your speech or read your essay are in your field. They know the standard information and data as well as you do. Avoid these practices, but be aware of them.

Also be aware of another practice: When an innovative writer or speaker comes up with a speech or article or essay that catches on, there'll be an epidemic of speeches, articles, and essays that are practically carbon copies of the original. In such instances, the process of developing standard information is speeded up.

When You Write Your Second Draft

Consider your first draft as inventory taking. When writing your second, consider alternative lead-writing techniques. Pick one that states your subject to best advantage, and with which you feel comfortable.

Use the ABC technique in presenting your documentation.

Make sure you have sentence-to-sentence and paragraph-to-paragraph continuity.

Don't do anything to make the reader stop and ask:

"Why is this pertinent to the subject or theme?"

Don't do anything to stop or slow down the illusion of forward movement.

Be sure you have stopped when you have finished.

The Next Step: Editing

In editing, the objective is to make sure you have touched all the bases outlined above.

Like inventory-taking, it's a step you can't afford to bypass.

We'll get into details in the next chapter.

Chapter 21

Editing: Insurance for Readers

"If you are particularly pleased with a sentence, strike it. Otherwise, arbitrarily eliminate every other sentence."

Those cynical comments contain truths that can't be ignored. In the light of second or third thought, yesterday's gem can be today's clinker.

The probability of such happenings and the desirability of catching them before they are thrust on the poor old reader suggest the desirability of putting your second draft aside and going to entirely different pursuits before you edit.

Time is an important factor. Two different frames of mind are involved. Writing is essentially a creative-critical process, with the former playing the lead role. Editing is, or should be, 100% critical.

Unless you are adept at method acting, it's difficult to switch from writer to editor (a disinterested second party). At the least, you have to get far enough away from writing to forget about it — overnight, for example.

A cooling-off period is a necessity because:

1 Pride of authorship must be overcome. Immediately after giving your paper or article your best shot, you have a natural feeling of elation; your self-confidence is high; you congratulate yourself with something like, "As of this moment, this is the best I can do."

2 At the same time, there is something of a letdown, and you are tired of what you have been writing. This climate does not favor editing.

3 Even if you force yourself to edit immediately after writing, chances are you won't be as open-minded as you should be. In writing, we develop a single-mindedness. After rewriting a sentence 12 times, you conclude you have found the only conceivable way of doing it. The same applies to your statement of the subject or theme, your choice of lead technique, your selection of key points, the telling devices used, and so on. In effect, the floor is no longer open for suggestions.

Those precautions are cited because the writer and editor are two different persons.

The editor is a critic.

He doesn't believe anything he reads.

He questions everything he reads.

He reads word for word, sentence for sentence.

He checks thinking.

He checks facts.

He checks development.

He checks continuity.

He checks judgment.

He checks language.

He is not an interested reader.

In fact, the moment the editor becomes a reader, he ceases to be an editor.

Finally, the editor is looking out for the reader — making sure that something worthwhile is said in a reasonable fashion.

It's good practice to have someone else give your masterpiece a critical look, but delay this until you have taken a crack at it. It'll help your development as a writer.

There is a technique that will help you change roles.

Simply put, "read the copy cold." Start editing beginning with the first word.

With this technique, you are duplicating the reader's experience. You are his policeman.

This technique avoids the pitfalls of a common practice, "read it through first before editing."

Here's what can happen if you peek before you edit.

Say the statement of the subject is buried in the third paragraph, while there is no reason why it shouldn't be in the first paragraph.

You'll see this if you read before you edit, but you'll tend to say,

"It'd probably be better in the first paragraph, but the reader will find it. I'll leave it where it is. The reader won't have to wait too long."

What we overlook or discount is that the reader does not have the benefit of this knowledge. He'll be puzzled and annoyed until he reaches the third paragraph.

Or say you run into a fuzzy statement in the second paragraph that is cleared up two paragraphs later.

Again, you'll tend to be forgiving.

So read it cold.

In assuming the reader's role, you'll probably spot the same chuckholes he would. Stop to repair each one before proceeding.

But don't piddle around with changes. Some authors, for example, will rewrite a sentence merely because they see another way of doing it. Leave it alone unless you can do better. Any sentence can be written at least a dozen different ways.

Also avoid a type of editing single-mindedness. The problem arises if you do not have a plan of attack or a procedure to follow.

Here's what happens. You read word-for-word until you find your first problem, say something like a switch from present to past tense. From that point on, you'll tend to be looking for that type of mistake to the exclusion of other types.

Also, like the writer, the editor normally reaches a point where he gets too close to what he is doing to make further headway.

Two readings — with a cooling-off period in between — are recommended. In each reading, you should be looking for specific things.

The checklists that follow, or reasonable facsimiles, should become part of your discipline.

Topics for the First Reading

There is no magic in what follows. The topics merely indicate the size of the ballpark and suggest a procedure and a rough order.

Look for big items the first time around, such as:

Is the subject or theme stated clearly?
Does the lead sound interesting?
If it's a special-purpose lead, is it tailored properly?
Is the lead the first element?
Should an alternative lead technique be considered?
Can the statement of the lead be speeded up?

Is the subject or theme buried?
Does direct documentation start immediately after the lead?
Can the transition from the lead to documentation be improved?
Is the documentation convincing?
Is each point developed in depth?
If tailoring is involved, is it handled properly?
Any gaps in logic or fact in the documentation?
More documentation needed?
Any evidence of telling about?
Need any information or data to fill gaps?
Any problems with pertinence?
Any problems with progression?
Is secondary documentation at the end?
Can any or all of the secondary documentation be dropped?
Is the paper, article, or speech too long?
Are you still convinced it is worthwhile?
Does it stop where it should?

Comment: Opinions on the need for formal endings vary. One camp maintains, "Just stop where you finish, but make sure you stop." The other side feels that a piece is incomplete if it doesn't have an ending. If you lean in the latter direction, you aren't faced with a major new requirement. Endings are easy. Merely repeat or paraphrase your title or the statement of your lead. Say you do a piece on "how to make a canoe in your attic." When you reach the end, you merely come up with something like "And that, folks, is how you make a canoe in your attic."

Topics for the Second Reading

Items in the preceding checklist can be assimilated with less trouble than it may appear, because they generally follow key steps in the writing process.

Not so for the following items. The second reading is a mop-up operation by nature; and it consists of a potpourri no reasonable person would attempt to learn by rote.

The items are listed in the sense of "be aware of things like this," and not in any order of importance:

Needless repetition.
Profound statements of the obvious.
Indirectness.

Words that don't inform.
Questions — direct or indirect — left unanswered.
Marginal or dubious information that should be deleted.
Typographical errors.
Grammatical errors.
Misspelled personal names.
Misspelled company names.
Misspelled cities or states.
Mistakes in arithmetic.
Mistakes in proportion.
Mistakes in fact.
Mistakes in logic.
Comparisons that can get you into trouble, or are at least unfair.
Overstatements that require toning down.
Understatements that should be jazzed up.
Anything else you missed in the first reading.

A Few Reminders

Remember, when editing you are a critic, not a writer, not an interested reader. You are a disinterested second party divorced from the writer.

Don't let the magic of the written word trap you.

For example, anything surrounded by quotation marks looks official and inviolable. But authorities can make the same mistakes in fact and logic as you do. They can even be devious — in quotes.

In editing, follow hunches.

If you see a red flag, stop, look, investigate.

Never make a change unless it is for the better.

Be a good housekeeper. Don't settle for less than clean, easy-to-read copy. Double space. Make corrections between the lines — horizontally, not vertically in the margins, or part horizontally and part vertically.

Chapter 22

What You Read Can Help You Write

There are at least two major differences between learning to ride a bicycle and learning to write.

Once you've mastered balancing, pedaling, and steering, you have gained and will retain enough proficiency to ride a bike even when you give it a try after a hiatus of ten years.

With proper application and desire, you can acquire the fundamentals of writing in a reasonable amount of time. But that's where the analogy to bicycling ends.

First, you must keep at writing to maintain the required state of mind or mental discipline. Professionals notice this on Monday morning after a weekend layoff. Getting back into gear after vacation can be murder.

Second, there are many degrees of writing proficiency. If you have bona fide pride of authorship, you'll never stop learning as long as you write.

The situation suggests a seldom-used technique that can aid and abet your development.

Look upon what you admire as a reader (newspapers, magazines, books, advertisements, anything) as living textbooks.

Read as a writer.

The idea is to peek over the author's shoulder.

Locate his lead.

What type of lead did he use?

How long did it take him to state it?

Do you disagree with anything so far?

Any tips you can use?

How does he make his transition from his lead to the start of his documentation?

Does he use incidents, case histories, examples, dialog, or quotes in his documentation?

How many major points does he cover?

Were any overdeveloped? Underdeveloped?

In your opinion, were any major points omitted?

Does he use a formal ending? How does he do it?

Once you pick up some proficiency with the above exercise, add the following items, or others like them:

Watch for how the author gets sentence-to-sentence continuity. Always ask: "Would I do it differently?"

Watch for strong adjectives and verbs. Note how much they contribute.

Watch for use of exact names, exact numbers, exact words. Note how they contribute.

Watch for signs of restraint — where the author could have gone overboard in making a critical point. (Generally, less is more.)

Watch for the use of third person, second person, first person. Think about the advantages and disadvantages of each in terms of what the author is doing.

Watch for ways to talk about things through people, incidents, and other devices.

Watch how statistics and statisticlike information are handled.

Watch for examples of the light touch. Situations in which the author uses a broad brush instead of going into needless and boring detail.

Watch for language devices. The simile, metaphor, synecdoche, euphemism, and so on.

Finally, in your must-reading at work, be particularly aware of all undesirable influences.

Remember, any form of "copying," whether it's a widely used ready-made outline or merely something you or someone else has written on a previous occasion, can have negative impacts on organization and content.

Remember, any language precedent that looks right or sounds right because of universal usage can have negative impacts on quality of content and the manner in which you write.

And that, folks, is how you can learn to write *what*.